D0596333

BRUCE WEBER'S
★ INSIDE ★
PRO FOOTBALL
1986

SCHOLASTIC INC.
New York Toronto London Auckland Sydney

PHOTO CREDITS

Cover: Focus on Sports. **2, 50:** Seattle Seahawks. **3, 40:** Pittsburgh Steelers. **4, 12, 13, 20, 44:** Los Angeles Raiders. **5, 11, 14, 16, 66:** Chicago Bears. **6, 82:** Atlanta Falcons. **7, 18, 30:** New England Patriots. **8, 58:** Washington Redskins. **9, 10, 24, 26:** Miami Dolphins. **15, 28:** New York Jets. **17, 46:** Denver Broncos. **19, 54, 56:** New York Giants. **21, 22, 76:** San Francisco 49ers. **23, 62:** Philadelphia Eagles. **32:** Indianapolis Colts. **34:** Buffalo Bills. **36:** Cincinnati Bengals. **38:** Cleveland Browns. **42:** Houston Oilers. **48:** San Diego Chargers. **52:** Kansas City Chiefs. **60:** Dallas Cowboys. **64:** St. Louis Cardinals. **68:** Detroit Lions. **70:** Green Bay Packers. **72:** Minnesota Vikings. **74:** Tampa Bay Buccaneers. **78:** Los Angeles Rams. **80:** New Orleans Saints.

Scholastic Books are available at special discounts for quantity purchases for use as premiums, promotional items, retail sales through specialty market outlets, etc. For details contact: Special Sales Manager, Scholastic Inc., 730 Broadway, New York, NY 10003, (212) 505-3346.

ISBN 0-590-40421-0

Copyright © 1986 by Scholastic Books, Inc.
All rights reserved. Published by Scholastic Inc.

12 11 10 9 8 7 6 5 4 3 2 1   10   6 7 8 9/8 0 1/9

CONTENTS

INTRODUCTION:
The Road to Pasadena

Super Bowl XXI must be better. The last edition, following nearly a week of parties in New Orleans, turned into a super cure for sleeplessness. Could you blame anyone (except a Bears' fan) for dozing off during the 46–10 demolishing of the Patriots last January?

The Bears were, simply, awesome. True, the AFC had at least a couple of teams that might have given Chicago a bigger challenge. The Miami Dolphins (the only team to beat the Bears all year) and the Los Angeles Raiders might well have been better opponents. But the Pats beat both of them along the way and earned their trip to Louisiana.

It's doubtful, however, that even an AFC All-Star team could have derailed the Bears. Jim McMahon threw beautifully, Willie Gault didn't drop the ball, Walter Payton and Matt Suhey found every hole, and the defense was incredible. The Pats' 10 points were the only points scored by Chicago opponents during the postseason. Go, Fridge!

So much for 1985. No matter what they do, the Bears will be back in the hunt in '86. Residing in one of the NFL's weakest divisions and owning one of the easiest schedules in the league (based on 1985 performances), Mike Ditka's boys will breeze into the play-offs. Another super trip, however, is not a sure thing.

First, repeat titles in sport are about as common as whooping cranes. Fact is, they occur more frequently in football than in baseball or basketball. Still, no team has made a repeat visit since San Francisco in Super Bowls XVII and XVIII, and the last repeat victors were the Steelers in Supes XIII and XIV. Why? No one really knows, but words like *incentive* and *motivation* are most frequently mentioned.

One more thing: Despite Ditka's denials, no one really knows how important defensive boss Buddy Ryan was in the Bears' success. Ryan is now in the head coach's office in Philadelphia, looking to settle the war of words when the Eagles visit the Bear den in the second week of the new season.

So we'll go with an upset in the NFC. Figuring that Lawrence Taylor has his head on straight, that Joe Morris will continue to pile up chunks of rushing yardage, and that Phil Simms will continue to throw the ball as well as anyone in the league, we'll take the New York Giants.

The New Yorkers (who play in New Jersey, of course) haven't played for a league title since losing to the Bears in the 1963 NFL championship game. They'll meet the same team in the 1986 NFC title game, and this time the result will be different.

Their Super Bowl XXI opponent will be the home team, the Los Angeles Raiders.

Though the Raiders play their home games in the L.A. Coliseum, about 10 miles west of Pasadena's Rose Bowl, they'll be quite comfortable, thank you, right in their own neighborhood.

The Raiders' road to Pasadena should be somewhat easier than the Giants'. They'll have to shut down Miami's Dan Marino to earn the crosstown trip. Their defense is quite capable of doing it. The major question is the Raider passing game. We believe that Al Davis will think of somthing.

The TV people are rooting for our folks. Can you imagine the extra viewers in the two biggest TV markets, New York and L.A., if the locals are playing for the big one? It'll be a blast! Enjoy.

— Bruce Weber

National Football League All-Pro Team

Wide Receiver
STEVE LARGENT
SEATTLE SEAHAWKS

The folks at the Pro Football Hall of Fame in Canton, Ohio, are dusting off a corner for Steve Largent. Despite limited size and limited speed, the sure-handed Largent has become one of the all-timers in the receiving department. He's certain to become Seattle's first Hall of Famer. What 'Hawk fans hope, of course, is that he won't be using that spot soon.

There are plenty of flashier performers in the NFL, but few are as steady as the former fourth-round draft choice of the Houston Oilers. A solid citizen in his Tulsa U. college days, Largent is one of the truly nice people in the pros. He gets plenty of respect and gives plenty, too.

Toward mid-October of this season, and barring anything we can't foresee, Largent will break Harold Carmichael's record of at least one catch in 127 straight games. But one usually isn't Steve's number. Last year, at age 31, he registered his seventh 1,000-yard season (an all-time record) and his eighth straight with 50 or more catches (another NFL mark). He wound up with 79 receptions for 1,287 yards (the league's best). If he stays in one piece, the 5–11, 184-pounder should own the whole record book someday.

Wide Receiver
LOUIS
LIPPS
PITTSBURGH STEELERS

In the steel city of Pittsburgh, they admire size. The quality of a man (and, especially, a football player) is measured by the bulk of his biceps.

Except for Louis Lipps. The slithery-quick third-year Steeler has created a storm of fan support, simply by doing shocking things on a football field. These include, of course, making catches normally rated impossible for a human and zipping through holes that aren't there while toting the best piece of leather the Wilson Company can produce.

"You simply don't believe him," says rival safety Deron Cherry of the Kaycee Chiefs. "The ball is thrown way downfield and you have a tendency to say overthrown. But Lipps gets to it. Impossible!"

Steeler offensive coordinator Tom Moore is in love with his little (5–11, 186) package of dynamite from Southern Mississippi. "He's a real quality person," says Moore. "All of us are lucky to be around him."

There were some doubters that Louis could repeat his 1984 Rookie of the Year numbers (45 receptions, 860 yards, 9 TDs) in '85. He simply buried them (59 catches, 1,134 yards, 12 scores). This season might be even better.

3

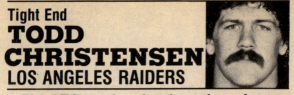

Tight End
TODD CHRISTENSEN
LOS ANGELES RAIDERS

The AFC easily rules the tight end roost. For years, the Chargers' Kellen Winslow was the man against whom all TEs were measured. With Winslow still battling back from a crippling injury, the title has passed — to Cleveland's super Ozzie Newsome and our choice for '86, the Raiders' Todd Christensen.

A failure as a running back (one year on the Cowboys' reserve list and one game in the Giants' backfield), Christensen came to the Raiders in 1979 and became a tight end. The 30-year-old from Brigham Young is L.A.'s possession receiver, the guy they go to when they need the key yards for a first down.

The 6–3, 230-pounder has been the club's top receiver for four straight seasons. His 82 receptions (for 987 yards and six TDs) in '85 marked his third consecutive season with 80 or more catches. No one in NFL history can make that claim.

Christensen, who amazes TV viewers with his tremendous intelligence off the field, impresses everyone on the field, too. He'll be looking for his fourth straight trip to the Pro Bowl after the '86 season. We'll be shocked if the Raiders' No. 3 all-time leading receiver doesn't make it.

Tackle
JIM COVERT
CHICAGO BEARS

Jim Covert has grown up. U. of Pitt fans remember him just a few years ago as Jimbo Covert. Not mature enough for a professional. So now he's Jim Covert. And at age 26 and starting his fourth NFL season, he has rapidly become the league's top offensive tackle — and one of the youngest team captains ever!

There's no secret about Covert's ability. The Bears know it. (He's one of the key reasons — along with a couple of talented backs, including Walter Payton — why the Bears owned the league's top rushing record a year ago.) The opponents know it, too. (The Los Angeles Raiders' tough defensive end, Howie Long, calls Covert just about the toughest guy he has faced.)

Jim possesses the great size and strength needed to excel as an outstanding offensive tackle. At 6–4 and 271, he's the perfect bookend, squeezing opposing defenders out of the way. During the NFC play-offs, he limited the Giants' premier pass-rusher, Leonard Marshall, to only one tackle and one assist. Giant fans were very impressed.

A college teammate of Miami QB star Dan Marino, Covert, in his own quiet way, is becoming a star equal to his more famous college buddy.

BILL FRALIC

ATLANTA FALCONS

This selection is a bit of a gamble. With so many great veteran tackles around the NFL, like the Bengals' Anthony Munoz, the Colts' Chris Hinton, the Rams' Jackie Slater, and the Patriots' Brian Holloway, it's hard to predict instant stardom for a second-year player.

Still, although we might be a year or two early, we believe that the ex-Pitt Panther, all 6–5, 280 pounds of him, will someday be the standard for NFL linemen.

Trouble is, Fralic may make it at guard or tackle, but it will take a better performance than 4–12 by the Falcons to prove it. Drafted as a tackle, Bill was switched to guard because of a shortage on the Atlanta front wall during training camp. By midseason, however, additional injuries had him back at his old college spot. He thrived in both positions, which gives the Falcons great flexibility for years to come.

Fralic fans (and the club is growing) point to Gerald Riggs's 1,719 rushing yards (best in the NFC) as proof of Fralic's ability. Though Atlanta suffered too many quarterback sacks, Fralic drew high marks from the entire Falcon coaching staff for his play as well as his willingness to do what had to be done.

Guard
JOHN HANNAH
NEW ENGLAND PATRIOTS

Despite the high of his first AFC title and first Super Bowl appearance, you couldn't blame John Hannah for spending the off-season studying his Blue Cross insurance coverage. At age 34, and starting his fourteenth NFL season, John Hannah remains the NFL'S top offensive guard and everyone's All-Pro choice. But his 1985 injury record would make a lesser man cry.

The 6–3, 265-pounder, called by at least one expert the greatest offensive lineman of all time, suffered from (1) a preseason calf strain, (2) the flu, (3) a pulled shoulder muscle, (4) a ruptured shoulder tendon. He missed a few outings along the way. But when he was in there, he never failed to play up to his usual All-Pro standards.

Possibly the biggest beneficiary of Hannah's super play was Craig James. A good running back, James became a real NFL star, running behind the former U. of Alabama stick-out.

In a sport laden with highly competitive types, Hannah ranks near or at the top. He's a rough, tough, hard-nosed player who's great blocking straight ahead and even better when he's pulling out to lead the way.

It's hard to tell how much longer Hannah can continue, but he remains our choice.

7

Guard
RUSS GRIMM
WASHINGTON REDSKINS

Ask Redskin fans to come up with one word to describe guard Russ Grimm and the answer heard most often is, "Solid!"

With his teammates dropping like flies around him (only three 'Skins started every game on offense), Russ continued to play at the highest level. For him, that means All-Pro. You know, solid!

A one-time Pitt Panther star, Grimm took over as a rookie (1981) and promises to stay a long time. Why not? He has all the tools. He's strong, tough, and, especially, durable. With 67 straight starts under his belt, you can always count on Russ being there on Sunday. Not that he isn't playing hurt some of the time. Washington line boss Joe Bugel say, "Russ has . . . an unbelievable knack of playing with injuries."

The Redskins credit the 6–3, 275-pound original Hog with the key blocks that sprang Washington backs for 157.7 yards per game on the ground in '85, the NFL's second-highest (behind Chicago) total. Redskin backs rushed for more than 100 yards eight times, a club record. Again credit goes to the 27-year-old former third-round draft pick. Most of Washington's two-time Super Bowlers are gone, but Grimm remains the rock of the offensive unit.

Center
DWIGHT STEPHENSON
MIAMI DOLPHINS

You usually don't hear much about centers. By being an All-Pro on a super team for years, Pittsburgh's Mike Webster became almost a household word. Before that, Oakland's Jim Otto was considered the best for about a decade. The Bears' Jay Hilgenberg finally got some recognition last year, thanks, in some measure, to Chicago's great year. But centers are usually blank faces (and blank names).

Enter Dwight Stephenson. If quarterback Dan Marino doesn't take the Dolphins' pivot man out to dinner at least once a week, he should. Dwight does an incredible job of keeping opponents off Dandy Dan's back, allowing him to find Mark Duper or Mark Clayton or some other mark, downfield.

Stephenson, now in his seventh pro season, has set the pace for NFL centers. He's imposing at 6–3 and 256 pounds, though not nearly as large as some of the guards and tackles who surround him. He's strong, make no mistake about it. But his strong suit is his amazing quickness.

Miami nose tackle Mike Charles is a big Stephenson fan. "I look forward to game days," he says. "That means I don't have to contend with Dwight, like I do in practice."

Quarterback
DAN
MARINO
MIAMI DOLPHINS

Okay, students. Take out your papers and pencils. This is a pop quiz. Only one question. Which statement is correct? (a) Dan Marino is football's top quarterback because his Miami team has no real running game; or (b) Miami has no real running game because all they need is valuable Dan Marino at quarterback.

Just to prove what easy graders we are, the good news is that both answers are somewhat correct. Congratulations!

It's tough to find fault with Miami coach Don Shula, one of the game's few living legends. He knows as well as anyone that rival defenses are stacked to stop Marino and his receiving corps. He also knows that his rushers don't scare anyone. And though he'd like to achieve a balanced offense, he can't ignore the fact that over the past two seasons, Marino has thrown 698 completions for 9,221 yards and 78 touchdowns. Despite a summer and early-season holdout, the 6–4, 210-pound three-year vet still led the league in TDs and yards. (His 21 interceptions were cause for concern, however.)

With his receivers healthy, there's no reason to believe that Marino won't continue as the NFL's No. 1 rifleman.

Running Back
WALTER PAYTON
CHICAGO BEARS

In the Chicago Bears' locker room, where seldom was heard a discouraging word last fall, "Sweetness" Payton seemed a little miffed. When the Super Bowl produced a 46–10 Bear win — but no TDs or real TD opportunities for the 11-year veteran — Walter was, shall we say, disappointed.

Still, as his reputation has always shown, he'll be back for another go-round as the Bears' top rusher *and* receiver. And that's good enough for us to name him to our All-Pro team again.

Sometime in the first or second week of the season, the 5–10, 200-pounder from Jackson State will tote the ball over the 15,000-yard mark. Someone will have to play well, long, and healthy to match that mark. And at age 32, having lost none of his skills, it's likely that Walter will tack another few thousand yards onto his total.

Payton may well duplicate his 1985 performance in '86. He had ten 100-yard games (including nine in a row, setting a since-tied NFL record). He enjoyed his third straight season with 2,000 or more yards of rushing and receiving (another record). And he caught 49 passes, 14 better than No. 2 teammate Emery Moorehead. The man is, simply, outstanding!

Running Back
MARCUS ALLEN
LOS ANGELES RAIDERS

Pin Al Davis down (not easy) and you will probably get the Los Angeles Raiders' owner to admit that his club's offense is spelled M-A-R-C-U-S A-L-L-E-N.

Sure, the offensive line does a fairly good job. And the gimpy quarterbacks have a corps of solid receivers. But Marcus Allen, the 6–2, 202-pounder from Southern Cal, is the key to it all. And as Allen goes, so go the Raiders.

Last season offered a perfect example. Both Allen and the team struggled early. But with a quarter of the season gone, the 25-year-old Allen bloomed, getting 100 yards or more in 11 of the last 12 Raider outings, including a record-tying nine in a row as the season ended. He finished atop the league with 1,759 rushing yards. Add in 555 yards on 67 receptions and his total yards from scrimmage (2,314) easily topped the Rams' Eric Dickerson's year-old NFL all-time mark.

"I did what I had to do," remembers Marcus. "Our quarterbacks [Jim Plunkett and Marc Wilson] were hurting, so I had to carry the ball." (His rushes per game zoomed from 17 to 24 in '85.) "That's what team play is all about, especially in Raider country." Al Davis wouldn't have it any other way.

Defensive End
HOWIE LONG
LOS ANGELES RAIDERS

Lots of football fans, overcome by the Raiders' bad-guy image, always believed that Howie Long was some kind of outlaw. Then came the feature last summer in *Sports Illustrated* that painted a remarkable picture of this remarkable athlete. Overcoming a less-than-healthy neighborhood environment in Boston, Long had put his life in good order. Now, the readers realized, he was only a "killer" on the field.

The 6–5, 270-pound monster has helped change the nature of defensive ends. Thanks to his spectacular play, particularly against the run, the experts are beginning to refer to DEs as skill position players. That title was formerly reserved for backs and ends and some linebackers. But Long has become an artist at the end of the line, much to the regret of Raider rivals.

Starting his sixth pro season, Long has become one of those "automatics." When you begin writing down your All-Pro lineup, you start with just a few "sure things." Howie Long is one of them.

Though he's not a sacker in the mold of the Jets' Mark Gastineau, Long is a more complete player. Watch for Raider opponents to go opposite the Long side, no matter what side that is!

Defensive End
RICHARD DENT
CHICAGO BEARS

Memo to Bear boss Mike McCaskey: Whatever you do and no matter what it costs, make certain that Richard Dent shows up in a Bear uniform every Sunday.

We believe that Richard, that 6–5, 263-pound wonder, is the key to the Chicago defense. It was defense, above all else, that made the Bears pro football's monstrous No. 1 team a year ago. Starting his fourth pro season, Dent is a regular on the All-Pro team. He never fails to set goals for himself — and never fails to reach them.

The only goal Dent had not achieved by Super Bowl time last January was financial. He even threatened to skip the big one to make clear his money target. (He also began negotiating with the USFL's New Jersey Generals this spring.)

Losing Dent would be a mistake for the Bears. His 17 sacks last season led the NFL. Then he added 4½ more (3½ on the Giants' Phil Simms) in the NFC play-offs. Out of respect to New England fans, we won't even mention the Super Bowl.

If pressure is the name of the defensive game, Dent is the clear-cut leader. He forces fumbles, recovers fumbles, tips passes. He does it all. At age 26, he should do the job for the next 10 years or so.

14

Nose Guard
JOE KLECKO
NEW YORK JETS

When we decided to go with a 3–4 defensive alignment on our All-Pro roster, we eliminated a couple of outstanding tackles, like Dallas's Randy White and Chicago's Steve McMichael. But when we looked at the nose guards, we knew we had to have the Jets' Joe Klecko on our team.

When Jet defensive boss Buddy Carson decided to switch the club to the 3–4, he gambled that Klecko could make the adjustment to the middle. Carson's gamble paid off. Klecko, who'll be 33 at midseason, stayed healthy through most of the season, and became a dominant defensive force. After registering only three sacks in '84, Joe bounced back with 7½ in '85 and quickly proved that he could deal well with the heavy traffic flow that overcomes many nose guards.

The change seemed to improve Joe's attitude, too. A former defensive end and tackle, Joe played with great enthusiasm throughout the season, leading the Jets into the play-offs. His unique playing style, setting up either right or left of the offensive center, helps him create all sorts of problems for Jet opponents. If he can avoid the knee problems that have dogged him in the past, he should remain a force.

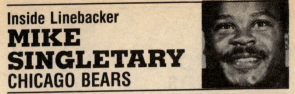

Inside Linebacker
MIKE SINGLETARY
CHICAGO BEARS

Now that defensive whiz Buddy Ryan is off to coach the Philadelphia Eagles (apparently taking the Bears' famed 46 defense with him), what's to become of Mike Singletary? Answer: nothing, really. Singletary should remain the imposing force that scares Chicago opponents to death.

Off the field, Mike assumes a relaxed pose, almost gentle. On the field, he's something else — a head-cracking, bone-crushing punishing machine. Forget the 46 defense. It's people, not systems, that make for tough defense, and Singletary will continue to provide that for the Bears.

The compact 6–0, 228-pounder made the big adjustment from Baylor Bear to Chicago Bear. He was always unstoppable against the run. It took a while before he matched that performance against the pass. Once he mastered that art, it wasn't surprising that he took his place on the All-Pro team.

The Bears' No. 2 tackler last year (with 113), they'll never forget him in Green Bay. He flattened 14 Packers in one game last November. A hard hitter who hates cheap shots and cheap-shot artists, Mike is rapidly reaching the status once given only to Dick Butkus in Chicago.

Inside Linebacker
KARL MECKLENBURG
DENVER BRONCOS

Sorry, fans of the Giants' Harry Carson, the Jets' Lance Mehl, and others. We love your guys. But this time around, we're putting our money on Denver's "man possessed," Karl Mecklenburg. The 6–4, 250-pounder from the U. of Minnesota was a dominating force on the tough Bronco defense a year ago, and the 26-year-old should pick up the beat again this season.

Actually, the fourth-year Bronco has played everywhere on the Denver defense (well, almost). It's a real surprise that he's playing anywhere. Anytime a twelfth-round draft pick qualifies for an All-Pro team, it's a shock. It was just a matter of Karl finding his spot. A decent enough defensive lineman, Meck really blossomed when he was shifted to linebacker. Denver coaches are convinced that he can be an even better linebacker once he really learns the position.

This is not good news to Denver opponents. The Raiders' Howie Long, who should know, calls Karl the league's best inside 'backer right now. That's pretty decent praise. Despite a team-high 13 sacks in '85, Meck confesses, "I don't always know what I'm doing out there." Oof! More bad news for Bronco rivals: He's learning!

Outside Linebacker
ANDRE TIPPETT
NEW ENGLAND PATRIOTS

Though he's considerably smaller (at 6–3, 241) than wrestler Andre the Giant, Andre the Patriot stands tall in the New England defensive force. When it comes to destroying enemy quarterbacks, Tippett does more sacking than an Idaho potato farmer. He added 16½ sacks in '85 to his 23½ in '84, making him the game's No. 1 sacker over the past two seasons.

Andre, who grew up in a tough Newark, New Jersey, neighborhood before making his way to the U. of Iowa, thirsts for recognition. "I always wanted to be considered in the class of Lawrence Taylor," Tippett recalls. Now, according to the experts, Andre may be even better.

Starting his fifth NFL season, Tippett has, indeed, risen to the top of his profession. The off-season karate expert is one of those kamikaze pass-rushers who'll go over or through anyone to get to the passer. Blessed with good quickness and outstanding strength, Andre is also known as one of the toughest guys in the league. He does nothing to deny that reputation.

"My goal," he says, "is to dominate on the field. I want to make things happen out there." Everyone in New England believes he has done it.

Outside Linebacker
LAWRENCE TAYLOR
NEW YORK GIANTS

Okay. We haven't learned our lessons. The slippage of pro basketballers like Michael Ray Richardson, John Lucas, and John Drew after "recovery" from substance problems is well known. So is Lawrence Taylor's 1986 off-season battle. Still, we believe that L.T. will bounce all the way back — which could produce the Giants' first division title in 23 years.

The Giants' 6–3, 243-pound defensive maniac was better than ordinary a year ago. But for him, ordinary is awful. It took the events of late winter and early spring to explain his so-so play.

The U. of North Carolina grad is still the fellow opposing offensive coaches have nightmares about during preparation week for the Giants. His ferocious pass-rushing usually requires a tackle, a back, and some prayer to stop. Few linebackers in the league pursue (come from the opposite side of the field) as well. And he's tough on pass coverage, too.

Giant fans (and Giant haters, too) will have their eyes on No. 56 this season. He knows that he let a lot of folks down in '85. We believe he'll have his head (and his helmet) on straight in '86, which means more sleepless nights for offensive coaches.

Cornerback
MIKE HAYNES
LOS ANGELES RAIDERS

Could the New England Patriots have done a better job in the Super Bowl with All-Pro Mike Haynes playing tough on the defensive corner? Probably. But, friends, it wouldn't have helped.

Fact is, Haynes, the former Patriot who left Foxboro, Massachusetts, in a contract squabble late in 1983, is doing just fine, thank you, with the Raiders in his hometown of Los Angeles. There's hardly ever a thought about the good (?) old days with the Pats.

Those who know the 6–2, 190-pound Haynes find it unusual for him to be succeeding with the hated Raiders. That fellow on the Raider helmet — the guy with the patch over one eye — is the Raider most people know. The tough guy, the guy you wouldn't invite to a nice party. A hard-nosed guy like Howie Long or the recently retired Lyle Alzado. Where, then, does gentleman Mike Haynes fit in?

"We're not really monsters," says Haynes, who's as tough on the run as he is on the pass. In a game that places a premium on hard hitting, the former Arizona State star gets his edge through preparation, thinking, and, for good measure, hard hitting, too.

Cornerback
ERIC WRIGHT
SAN FRANCISCO 49ERS

For years, NFL coaches looked for big cornerbacks, fellows in the 6–2, 6–3 range and weighing about 220 or so. For some time now, however, a new trend has developed: amazingly quick, small players, such as Washington's Darrell Green (5–8, 170), going against the new, quicker breed of receivers.

And then there's Eric Wright. When he and Ronnie Lott took over the corners for Bill Walsh's 49ers as rookies in 1981, they created a whole revolution in secondary play.

Lott has since been moved to safety, and the team continues to thrive. But it's Wright, all 6–1, 180 pounds of him, that combines the best of everything in a cornerback. Wright is both fast and strong, just what the doctor (even Dr. Walsh) ordered at the position. He's probably a bit better in pass-coverage situations than he is against the run. And though he didn't have his greatest season in '85 (the Cowboys' Everson Walls and the Rams' Leroy Irvin were most impressive), we'll make him our pick for '86.

NFL strategy experts quickly concede that a team cannot win without quality corner men. Eric Wright will put the 49ers at or near the top again.

Strong Safety
CARLTON WILLIAMSON
SAN FRANCISCO 49ERS

Picking an All-Pro strong safety may be the neatest trick of all. You can hardly go wrong with any of several super players.

The Seahawks' Ken Easley is the usual choice. But he had some bangs that limited him last year, and we'll have to see if he makes it all the way back. The St. Louis Cardinals were terrible, but their SS Leonard Smith was a standout almost every Sunday. And speaking of Smith, you could do a lot worse than Denver's Dennis Smith.

But our choice is San Francisco's six-year veteran, Carlton Williamson. Part of the amazing 1981 draft that also produced outstanding defensive backs Ronnie Lott and All-Pro Eric Wright, Williamson does everything coach Bill Walsh could ask. He's best when he gets his hands on the ball with running room. He turned three interceptions into 137 yards of returns, including one brilliant 82-yard TD scamper.

The 28-year-old is one of a batch of Pitt alumni on our 1986 All-Pro roster. His fellow Panthers include Bill Fralic, Dan Marino, Jim Covert, and Russ Grimm. Quite an alumni team! The 6–0, 204-pound Williamson may be the smallest of the group. But, as his 80 tackles last year prove, he's just as tough as any of them.

WES HOPKINS
PHILADELPHIA EAGLES

New Eagle coach Buddy Ryan has made his reputation on defense. It has to warm his heart knowing that he starts his new job with the best free safety in the business.

The 6–1, 212-pounder from SMU has plenty of fans — in addition to the thousands of Eagle rooters. His former coach, Marion Campbell, says, "Wes is an intimidator and a clean hitter all the way. He's a sure, sharp tackler who just loves to hit people. And when he hits you, you know you've been popped."

CBS-TV's (and former Chief coach) Hank Stram puts it a little sharper: "If Wes Hopkins isn't All-Pro, there ought to be an investigation."

No problem here, Coach. A great ball-hawk and a fine blitzer whenever Philadelphia brings a safety, Hopkins is the Eagles' tackling leader with 136 last year (including 71 solos) and their leading interceptor, too (with six).

Wes, who will turn 25 during the fourth week of the season, single-handedly dismantled the Cowboys in '85, with two interceptions (at the three and in the end zone) and a fumble recovery.

Now, if Buddy can find 10 more like Wes, he'll really have something.

A full-time, rifle-armed Dan Marino (and a healthy Mark Duper) should lead the Dolphins to the top of the AFC East.

American Football Conference Team Previews

AFC East
MIAMI DOLPHINS
1985 Finish: First
1986 Prediction: First

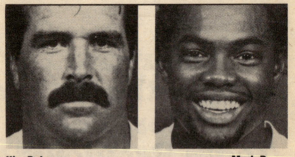

Kim Bokamper   **Mark Duper**

Great passing, adequate running, decent defense, and superlative coaching. That's the Miami Dolphins' formula. And as long as quarterback Dan Marino and coach Don Shula are on the scene, the Dolphins have to be the team to beat in the AFC East.

Though he didn't do as well as in '84, QB Marino proved he didn't need training camp to make it big in the NFL. With 254 completions for 4,137 yards and 30 TDs, Pittsburgh Dan became the fourth QB ever to throw for 30 TDs or more in consecutive seasons. Vet Don Strock is a solid backup.

Marino's passes must be caught, of course, and there are few receiver groups better than Miami's. The Marks brothers, Clayton and Duper, are dynamite. How the Dolphs missed Duper when he was out the first half of '85. Nat Moore is an excellent backup, and a healthy Tom Vigorito will help. TE Bruce Hardy comes back off his finest season, but subs Dan Johnson and Joe Rose are still question marks.

The best you can say for the runners is that they're dependable, none more so than Tony Nathan (143 carries for 667 yards, plus 72 receptions for 651 yards). Rookie Ron Davenport was a pleasant surprise as a real goal-line weapon, backing up Woody Bennett at fullback. Joe Carter and Lorenzo Hampton, neither a world-beater, back up Nathan.

Pro Bowlers C Dwight Stephenson and G Roy Foster held together an offensive line that made Marino the NFL's most protected passer. Jon Geisler and Cleveland Green show great promise at tackle. With Ed Newman just about finished, Ronnie Lee and Steve Clark will do battle at guard.

The defensive line, led by ends Doug Betters and Kim Bokamper and noseman Mike Charles, was okay. The return of Bob Baumhower will help. OLB Hugh Green fit in instantly, joining Bob Brudzinski, Mark Brown, and Jackie Shipp, along with Jay Brophy and Robin Sendlein at linebacker.

CB William Judson had a fine '85, and Paul Lankford filled in well for Don McNeal. S Glenn Blackwood must do better against the run and on man coverage. FS Bud Brown performed well enough to keep Lyle Blackwood on the sidelines.

AFC East
NEW YORK JETS
1985 Finish: Second
1986 Prediction: Second

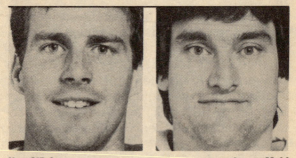

Ken O'Brien   **Lance Mehl**

The Jets broke more than a few hearts in the Big Apple in '85. First they blew an excellent opportunity to win a rare Eastern Division title, then they blew a home wild-card play-off game to New England.

The good news is that the Jets will have a great chance to make up for those failings in '86. QB Ken O'Brien, the NFL's top-rated passer, looks as if he's got what it takes to lead a championship team. He tossed up only eight intercepts in 16 games last year, the league's top figure. He must learn when to dump the ball off, however, to avoid some of the 62 sacks he suffered in '85.

RB Freeman McNeil ranks with the best when he's healthy — which isn't often enough. His slashing style, always headed upfield, leads to too many injuries. Still, his 1,331 yards (a 4.5 average) was second best in the AFC. Johnny Hector is a top backup. More depth is required here.

The addition of exciting Al Toon opened up things for WR Wesley Walker, giving the Jets explosive power on the outside. Meanwhile TE Mickey Shuler made 76 receptions, which was one of the top TE totals in the NFL. It's a fine trio.

Along with the defensive secondary, the offensive line is a major Jet problem. Neither LT, Reggie McElroy nor Ted Banker, could do the job, and RT Marvin Powell is gone. C Joe Fields was fine and the guards were okay, with Jim Sweeney just a bit better than Dan Alexander.

DE Mark Gastineau and NT Joe Klecko thrived in the Jets' new 3–4 defense in '85. There's no reason to believe they won't continue. Marty Lyons is particularly effective vs. the run, and Ben Rudolph and Barry Bennett both played well.

The linebacker corps could use some help on the outside, particularly by someone with speed. ILB Lance Mehl earned his Pro Bowl spot, and Kyle Clifton was an adequate inside mate. Charles Jackson did well on the outside.

Would that the defensive backfield did as well. But if the rash of injuries, which forced the Jets into all sorts of makeshift combinations, stops, the group could succeed. Look for Kerry Glenn and Bobby Jackson to continue their outstanding work.

AFC East
NEW ENGLAND PATRIOTS
1985 Finish: Third
1986 Prediction: Third

Brian Holloway   **Craig James**

In just a few days last January, the Cinderella Patriots suffered major damage to their glass slipper. The palace ball included three play-off victories and a trip to the Super Bowl.

Then came reality. The Chicago Bears struck 11:55 P.M. with their 46–10 whomping of the New Englanders. Midnight struck a couple of days later with the announcement of major drug problems.

We'll look at the '86 prospects under the assumption that everyone will be back and ready to go. Even so, a return Super Bowl visit is unlikely. The QB duo of Tony Eason and Steve Grogan is unlikely to repeat its "my turn, your turn" heroics of late '85.

The receivers are more likely to repeat, with Stanley Morgan and Irving Fryar giving New England its best deep threat in many years. Stephen Starring and Cedric Jones are excellent backups. Injuries make TE a question mark.

The running game is in excellent shape, thanks to the tandem of Craig James (1,227 yards) and Tony Collins (657 yards and 52 team-leading receptions). Mosi Tatupu is a top-flight blocker and short-yardage runner. Top pick Reggie Dupard of SMU is an excellent addition.

Any line featuring all-timer John Hannah, who played hurt much of the time, and Pro Bowler Brian Holloway can't be bad. A healthy Pete Brock at center should make things even better. Ron Wooten and Steve Moore anchor the right side.

A healthy Ken Sims should join with Garin Veris to lead the defensive line, though the Pats will miss retired Julius Adams. Lester Williams and Dennis Owens will battle for the starting NT spot.

The linebackers are outstanding, with All-Pro LOLB Andre Tippett (a conference-leading 16½ sacks) the best of a good lot. ROLB Don Blackmon really pressures rival QBs, and inside men Steve Nelson and Larry McGrew are fine. If Clayton Weishuhn is ready to go, this group will be even better.

Ronnie Lippett (say li-PET these days) and Raymond Clayborn both enjoyed fine years on the corners in '85, with FS Fred Marion (seven intercepts) and SS Roland James (four) absolutely solid.

AFC East
INDIANAPOLIS COLTS
1985 Finish: Fourth
1986 Prediction: Fourth

Vernon Maxwell **Ron Solt**

While most teams were preparing for the draft last spring, Colt owner Bob Irsay and wife Harriet were in divorce court, battling for ownership of the team. The joke in Indianapolis was that the loser would get control.

Not that the Colts are that bad. Off a 5–11 record in '85, there's some hope for this year. The club finished well, winning the last two after close losses to the Super Bowl teams, Chicago and New England.

Trouble is, the Colts' best player may be punter Rohn Stark, owner of a 45.9-yard average last year. The offensive line is outstanding, too. The key man is T Chris Hinton, one of the game's best. Ray Donaldson is fine at center with Ben Utt, Ron Solt, and Roger Caron at the guards. The return of T Jim Mills would help.

The running game is in fairly good shape. RB Randy McMillan closed fast to gain 856 yards. George Wonsley picked up another 716. Whenever the Colts won in '85, the rushing game accounted for 200 yards or more.

The passing game isn't nearly as effective. There are high hopes for ex-Cowboy Gary Hogeboom, obtained in a predraft trade. He should replace Mike Pagel, who threw only 14 TDs in '85 and tossed 15 interceptions, ranking twelfth in the AFC. The receivers aren't much either. Wayne Capers did well (17.5 yards per catch) with Matt Bouza on the opposite side. TE Pat Beach was the Colts' top catcher (only 36).

The return of vet NT Leo Wisniewski and DE Blaise Winter would strengthen a so-so defensive line. Top draftee Jon Hand will help, and improved Donnell Thompson is first-rate. Willie Broughton has a future at nose tackle, and Brad White, Chris Scott, and Scott Virkus should see plenty of action.

LB Duane Bickett could be an All-Pro soon. ILB Cliff Odom finally came into his own last year. Vets Johnnie Cooks and Barry Krauss should return to the lineup.

The AFC's co-leader in interceptions, CB Eugene Daniel, leads a much-improved Colt secondary. Leonard Coleman will battle for a starting CB berth with Preston Davis. Vet Nesby Glasgow and young (what else?) Anthony Young are the safeties.

AFC East
BUFFALO BILLS
1985 Finish: Fifth
1986 Prediction: Fifth

Charles Romes   **Greg Bell**

Possibly the Bills' greatest strength is its coaching staff. Hank Bullough, who took over from Kay Stephenson after the Bills went 0–4 early in '85, is first-rate. He has brought in four new assistants for '86, and that can only help.

Unfortunately, no coach has ever scored a touchdown, tackled a runner, or kicked a field goal. The problems are certainly on the field, and it will take some time to correct them.

Quarterback is the biggest problem. Bruce Mathison, who started the last seven games a year ago, shows good mobility, some promise, and a tendency to throw too many interceptions (14 against only four TDs). Rookie Frank Reich threw only one pass all season (completing it for 19 yards).

USFLer Jim Kelly (the Bills own his NFL rights) would certainly help.

Greg Bell figures to be the heart of the Bills' offense again. He led the team in rushing (883 yards), receiving (58 catches), and TDs (9) last year. FB Booker Moore has never really impressed, and the backups are ordinary. No. 1 draftee Ronnie Harmon of Iowa should fit right in.

The offensive line was greatly improved in '85 and there's future hope here, too. Look for Mark Traynowicz to push Will Grant at center. Tackles Joe Devlin and Ken Jones are first-rate, and guards Jim Ritcher and Tim Vogler are decent. Chris Babyar could challenge for a guard spot.

The defensive line should be a Bill bright spot. The top draftee in the '85 derby, Bruce Smith, showed flashes of greatness in his rookie year. But neither end Ben Williams nor noseman Fred Smerlas was up to previous standards. The return of injured Mike Hamby could help in the middle.

A healthy (for a change) Jim Haslett and Eugene Marve played well against the run from their ILB slots. Ex-Bengal Guy Frazier joins Lucius Sanford on the outside. There's decent depth in the linebacker crew, including ex-starter Darryl Talley.

Cornerback Charles Romes comes off his most productive season, featuring seven intercepts. He joins cornerman Derrick Burroughs and safeties Steve Freeman and Martin Bayless, with Rodney Bellinger ready for extra-back situations.

AFC Central
CINCINNATI BENGALS
1985 Finish: Second (tied)
1986 Prediction: First

Boomer Esiason   **James Brooks**

The interesting thing about the AFC Central is that the Bengals have won only 15 games (out of 32) the past two years but have been in the play-off hunt the last week of each season.

"In the hunt" isn't good enough this time around. With QB Boomer Esiason ready to go from the opening whistle, coach Sam Wyche figures the Bengals will bust right out of the gate. (Cincy has gone 1–7 during the opening month of the two previous seasons.)

Cincinnati's play-off hopes start with blond Boomer. The lefty from Maryland outdueled vet Ken Anderson and backup Turk Schonert (now gone) to win the starting nod, then threw for 27 TDs (three in a game six times) and 3,443 yards. He ranked second only to the Jets' Ken O'Brien.

Esiason has an outstanding group of receivers. Eddie Brown (a team-leading 17.8 yards per catch) had a fine rookie year. Cris Collinsworth (65 catches, 1,125 yards) is one of the NFL's best, and TEs Rodney Holman and M.L. Harris are fine.

The backfield depends on ex-Charger James Brooks (929 yards plus 55 pass receptions). If Larry Kinnebrew is in shape, he'll help. Charles Alexander may have trouble keeping his job.

There's plenty of talent on the offensive line, but the performance didn't match it. All-Pro Anthony Munoz is the force, along with Brian Blados, Dave Rimington, Mike Wilson, and Max Montoya. There's room for improvement here (too many sacks, not enough rushing yardage).

Ross Browner, back from the USFL, is the best-known Cincy pass-rusher. But NT Tim Krumrie really blossomed in '85. They'll be back, along with E Eddie Edwards.

The linebacking crew is led by Reggie Williams, whose nose for the football produced four fumble recoveries in '85. Carl Zander, Jeff Schuh, and Glenn Cameron should return. No. 1 pick Joe Kelly of Washington should see lots of action.

As for the secondary, Louis Breeden, Ray Horton, and Bobby Kemp all spent time in the doctor's office. FS James Griffin is the top interceptor. Wyche must make a major improvement here (ranked 26th in the league last year) for the team to move up.

AFC Central
CLEVELAND BROWNS
1985 Finish: First
1986 Prediction: Second

Tom Cousineau   **Ozzie Newsome**

With a solid defense and an outstanding running game, the Browns are two thirds of the way toward reaching the top level of NFL teams. The passing game, unfortunately, may keep them from reaching that goal in '86.

Bernie Kosar, the object of everyone's affections before the '85 season, shows promise. But it was ex-Lion Gary Danielson who gave the Browns whatever solid passing attack they had last year. Kosar, who had eight TDs among his 124 completions and 1,578 yards, is the QB of the future. That future, however, is probably not just yet.

The running game, on the other hand, is first-rate. Kevin Mack ran for 1,104 yards last year, with partner Earnest Byner racking up 1,002. That's the first time since 1976 that two teammates each crossed the 1,000-yard barrier. There's plenty of depth, too, with Curtis Dickey, Boyce Green, Greg Allen, and Johnny Davis.

In the receiving department, there are few pros in the class of TE Ozzie Newsome (62 catches for 711 yards). But the wide receivers, including starters Brian Brennan and Clarence Weathers and backups Fred Banks and Reggie Langhorne, aren't enough.

The offensive line, vastly improved in '85, has become an asset. RT Cody Risien is the leader, along with guards Dan Fike and George Lilja and center Mike Baab. Rickey Bolden is set at left tackle.

Noseman Bob Golic is a Pro Bowler, and there's plenty of pass-rush out of ends Carl Hairston and Reggie Camp. Overall, the Browns were excellent against the run. Dave Puzzuoli, Sam Clancy, and Keith Baldwin provide good backup.

Linebacking is in excellent hands. LOLB Chip Banks and RILB Tom Cousineau are among the league's best. LILB Eddie Johnson is excellent against the run. ROLB Clay Matthews is consistent.

Hard-hitting Al Gross and Don Rogers give the Browns the best pair of safeties in the AFC Central. Combined with corners Frank Minnifield and Hanford Dixon, this quartet makes beautiful music.

Now if there were only an easy way to spell coach Marty Schottenheimer's name.

AFC Central
PITTSBURGH STEELERS
1985 Finish: Second (tied)
1986 Prediction: Third

Tunch Ilkin   **Frank Pollard**

Tell a Steeler fan that you want to talk
football, and he'll probably want to talk
wide receivers. Not that the Steelers are
talentless, not that they don't get great
coaching, not that they couldn't surprise
some folks in the weak AFC Central. It's just
that Pittsburgh is coming off its first losing
season in 13 years, and there aren't a lot of
things worth discussing.

Wide receivers? Sure. Little Louis Lipps
is becoming an All-Pro, off 12 TD catches
and 15 TDs overall. Thirteen-year veteran
John Stallworth was sixth in the AFC in
receptions (75) but with only 12.5 yards per
catch (nearly five yards per catch less than
in '84). Calvin Sweeney is a good backup,
but there's need for new talent to spell
Stallworth.

The offensive line must stay healthy for the Steelers to improve. C Mike Webster, an all-timer, continues to do the job in the middle. Ex-USFLer Ray Pinney was a big plus at left tackle. Coach Chuck Noll should be able to find a spot for top draft pick John Rienstra of Temple.

A game-breaking running back is a primary need. Frank Pollard (991 yards) is solid, and Walter Abercrombie (851 yards) is okay, too. A healthy Rich Erenberg (a stick-out as a rookie in '84 but banged up most of '85) would help.

Mark Malone (117 completions, 13 TDs in 10 games) is probably the best of the QBs. David Woodley threw too many interceptions, and Scott Campbell isn't ready. This is a tough spot.

The defensive line produced only 36 sacks last season (after 47 the year before) and needs help. Left end Keith Willis was the top sacker (5½), while Edmund Nelson and Keith Gary should play on the right. NT Gary Dunn does well against the run when he's healthy, which isn't often enough.

OLB Mike Merriweather is the best of the Steeler LBs, with ILB Robin Cole still doing well. On the right outside, Bryan Hinkle is okay, but LILB David Little may not be up to Steeler standards.

In the backfield, a stronger pass-rush would probably remove some of the pressure. Though the Steelers allowed the fewest passing yards in the AFC, the group really didn't do the job.

AFC Central
HOUSTON OILERS
1985 Finish: Fourth
1986 Prediction: Fourth

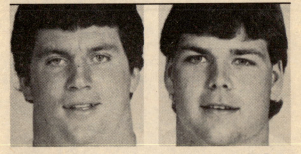

Mike Munchak   **Bo Eason**

Too many Houston fans find the Oilers offensive. The problem is their offense, which leaves much to be desired.

Now it's up to new coach Jerry Glanville to try to find the people to put points on the Astrodome scoreboard. With the defense in decent shape, an offensive turnaround would make the coach's years in Houston quite pleasant.

Trouble is, those folks don't seem to be available in east Texas. Despite a fast close (three 300-yard games), one-time Canadian QB star Warren Moon may never make a major impact on the NFL. In Moon's two years, he has thrown for 6,047 yards (2,709 last year) and 27 TDs (15 in '85). But he also tossed up 33 interceptions, including 19 last season. Purdue's Jim Everett, the Oilers'

No. 1 draft pick, may be ready soon.

The receiving corps deserves better. Ex-Ram Drew Hill proved an outstanding Oiler trade pickup, with 64 catches for 1,169 yards. WR Tim Smith closed fast, and TE Jamie Williams is reliable. RB Butch Woolfolk led the club in receptions with 80 for 814 yards.

But neither Woolfolk nor ex-USFLer Mike Rozier did anything memorable, and Larry Moriarty never recovered from his early-season holdout. The running game is a bummer.

The offensive line is in better condition. G Mike Munchak was a Pro Bowl starter, and Bruce Matthews and Harvey Salem are first-class. C Jim Romano is okay, but the jury is still out on former top draftee Dean Steinkuhler.

The defense is on the right path. DE Ray Childress, 1985's top draftee, keyed a renewed pass-rush, along with ex-USFL ace Doug Smith. Mike Stensrud is still solid. The Oilers need another end to go with Childress.

LB Frank Bush made an immediate impact as a rookie, along with Robert Abraham. Both always were around the ball. Avon Riley was the team's top tackler, and Robert Lyles played well. Another inside backer would help.

CB Steve Brown, with five interceptions, was one of the Oilers' defensive leaders. Patrick Allen will fight Richard Johnson at the other corner, with Keith Bostic and Bo Eason set as safeties.

AFC West
LOS ANGELES RAIDERS
1985 Finish: First
1986 Prediction: First

Henry Lawrence　　　　　　　　　　**Bill Pickel**

With a break in the health department
and solution to a weakness at quarterback, the Raiders should continue to dominate the AFC West. The team's third Super
Bowl victory in the eighties is not
impossible.

The Raider front office always seems to
have talented players to replace older
players. In '85 young Don Mosebar replaced
veteran center Dave Dalby. That helped
shore up the line, which still has tackles
Bruce Davis and Henry Lawrence and
guards Mickey Marvin and Charley Hannah. Curt Marsh, Shelby Jordan, and Dalby
are excellent reserves.

That group does an excellent job for QBs
Jim Plunkett (who missed most of '85 with
a shoulder injury) and six-year vet Marc

Wilson (who carried on in '85 despite a shoulder separation and a severe ankle sprain). Backup Rusty Hilger may still be a year or two away, and '85 injured reserve Russ Jensen is untested.

The running game is in able hands, led by All-Pro Marcus Allen, who enters this season with nine straight 100-yard games. With Frank Hawkins and Kenny King ready to go, there's plenty of depth.

The Raiders have always believed in the long pass, and there's enough speed to assure its continued use. Dokie Williams (48 catches, 925 yards) is the leader, along with second-year men Jessie Hester and Tim Moffett. All-timer Cliff Branch hasn't lost more than a half step.

L.A. will miss retired Lyle Alzado. But the Raiders are in excellent shape, with All-Pro Howie Long and second-year man Sean Jones at the ends and tough Bill Pickel in the middle. Look for Greg Townsend, Mitch Willis, and Elvis Franks to provide depth.

Rookie Reggie McKenzie was a big, pleasant surprise at an inside 'backer spot in '85. Matt Millen and Rod Martin are proven stars, and vet Brad Van Pelt has found a fountain of youth on the outside. A healthy Bob Nelson would make this group even better.

Cornerbacks Mike Haynes and Lester Hayes remain one of the NFL's top duos. Safeties Mike Davis and Vann McElroy should be healthy again. Young Stacey Toran will help everywhere.

AFC West
DENVER BRONCOS
1985 Finish: Second
1986 Prediction: Second

Rulon Jones   **Louis Wright**

Talk about bad timing. Despite an 11–5 record (good enough to win the title in the NFC East and AFC Central), the Broncos finished third in the battle for the two AFC wild-card berths. Will '86 be different? It's hard to tell.

Much depends on QB John Elway. The one-time Stanford ace started like a house afire in '85, then slumped late in the year. He ranked eighth among AFC passers, with a lower rating than in '84. There's no doubt that John has the tools, but he still has to prove himself.

If the Broncos can find a game-breaking pass receiver, Elway could be that much better. Still, there's plenty of strength on the outside, with Steve Watson (61 receptions) and young Vance Johnson (51). Johnson is quick, but more is needed. The tight end tandem of Clarence Kay and James Wright is excellent. They caught 57 balls between them. Clint Sampson provides fine support at WR where Butch Johnson has lost at least a step.

The running game is in decent shape. Sammy Winder finished with 714 yards (and eight TDs), despite missing nearly four full games. He should return to his usual 1,000-yard spot. Steve Sewell (275 yards) finished strong, and Gene Lang (318) is solid.

Up front, RG Paul Howard continues to do the job. RT Ken Lanier is a fine blocker, and T Dave Studdard and G Keith Bishop will hold down the left side. Billy Bryan is fine at center. Watch for Mark Cooper to get a shot at a guard spot.

The Orange Crush may well be back in the defensive line. RE Rulon Jones is ready to become an every-year Pro Bowler. He had 10 sacks a year ago. LEs Barney Chavous and Andre Townsend combined for another 11. Rubin Carter is a solid noseman.

All-Pro Karl Mecklenburg is a first-rate LILB who plays in the line on passing downs. He teams with Jim Ryan on the left side, with Steve Busick and Tom Jackson on the right.

All-timer Louis Wright mans the left corner, along with right corner Mike Harden, SS Dennis Smith, and FS Steve Foley. Smith's health is a key to this fine group's success. If ex-Giant All-Pro Mark Haynes bounces back, they'll be even better.

AFC West
SAN DIEGO CHARGERS
1985 Finish: Third (tied)
1986 Prediction: Third

Dan Fouts   **Lionel James**

The guy who runs the scoreboard at San Diego's Jack Murphy Stadium ought to ask for a raise. The Charger's electric offense and Swiss-cheese defense make for scoring fun-fests at San Diego games. Unfortunately, the Chargers often come out with the lower number. Last year was typical, with victories at 44–41, 40–34, and 54–44; and losses at 37–35, 49–35, and 38–34. Only a late-season rally (five wins in the last eight games) saved coach Don Coryell.

Once again the cry of "Dee-fense!" was heard, not at the stadium, but at draft headquarters. There are some pluses, including a decent pass-rush from DEs Lee Williams (nine sacks) and Fred Robinson. Chuck Ehin was okay at NT. Oklahoma State's Leslie O'Neal may be one of the answers up front. Inside backers Billy Ray Smith and Mike Green were the team's top tacklers. Woody Lowe and Linden King were okay on the outside, with help from Mike Guendling.

San Diego's secondary picked off most of the Chargers' 26 interceptions a year ago, including corners Danny Walters with five and John Hendy with four. But the group, including safeties Gill Byrd and Jeff Dale, allowed 28 TDs. Not good enough.

Offensively, there's plenty of firepower as long as QB Dan Fouts stays healthy. Fouts, who started only nine games, threw for 27 TDs and ranked third among AFC passers. Surprisingly, backup Mark Herrmann played well in relief, tossing 10 scoring passes. Combined, the duo threw for 37 TDs, leading the league.

Little 5–6 Lionel "Little Train" James sparked an exciting Charger running game. James rushed for 516 yards, caught an AFC-leading 86 passes for 1,027 yards, returned 25 punts for 213 yards, and brought back 36 kickoffs for 779 yards. A one-man wrecking crew is this ball of fire. Backfield mates Tim Spencer and Gary Anderson rushed for more than 900 yards combined.

The receivers, including James, wideout Wes Chandler (67 catches for 1,199 yards), TEs Pete Holohan and Eric Sievers, and recovered Kellen Winslow, are first-rate. Even ancient Charlie Joiner, an all-timer, had 59 catches and 932 yards.

AFC West
SEATTLE SEAHAWKS
1985 Finish: Third (tied)
1986 Prediction: Fourth

Curt Warner   **Jacob Green**

The toughest division in the NFL? AFC fans leave no doubt. It's the AFC West. Which means that it'll be harder than ever for the Seattle Seahawks to return to their old spot in the league play-offs.

Facing a super-tough schedule, coach Chuck Knox can only hope that his offense can increase its production and reduce its turnovers, two reasons why the 'Hawks finished out of the money in '85.

That puts extra pressure on new offensive coordinator Steve Moore. His line must be more consistent and reduce its sacks allowed. Center Blair Bush should return, along with guards Edwin Bailey and Robert Pratt and tackles Ron Essink and Bob Cryder. But expect Bryan Millard and Ron Mattes to get a long look early.

Interestingly, Seattle made the play-offs without superstar Curt Warner in '84, then gained fewer rushing yards and missed the play-offs with a recovered Warner in '85. Still, Curt gained 1,094 yards (but an unsatisfactory 3.8 yards per carry) and caught 47 passes for 307. Fullback is a problem area. David Hughes and Dan Doornink were hurt much of the year, and former Bronco Rick Parros, John Williams, and Eric Lane get a shot in '86.

WR Daryl Turner should become a superstar soon. All-Pro Steve Largent (79 catches, 1,287 yards) is one of the best — ever. Dan Ross may hold his TE spot.

Overall, the word in Seattle is: As QB Dave Kreig goes, so go the Seahawks. When he's good, they're very, very good; when he's bad, they just lose. He was intercepted twice in their eight wins last year, 18 times in the eight losses.

DE Jacob Green (13½ sacks) spearheads the adequate defensive line, along with DE Jeff Bryant, NT Joe Nash, and backup Randy Edwards. NT Reggie Kinlaw returns from the injured list. Pro Bowler Fredd Young is set at ILB along with vet Keith Butler. Seattle's run defense is suspect. Bruce Scholtz and Michael Jackson are the OLBs.

A healthy Ken Easley at strong safety will strengthen a strong defensive backfield. CB Dave Brown and FS John Harris are among the league's top interceptors. CB Terry Taylor rounds out the group and stars as a punt blocker.

AFC West
KANSAS CITY CHIEFS
1985 Finish: Fifth
1986 Prediction: Fifth

Lloyd Burruss   **Carlos Carson**

One of the major surprises of the off-season was the continued presence of John Mackovic in the coach's office. Actually, the one-time Dallas assistant does a pretty fair job. A quick start in '86 would help his job security. Unfortunately, his Chiefs reside in the rough, tough AFC West, where 11-5 Denver missed the play-offs.

Kaycee was nowhere in the 11-5 class. With no running game and a so-so defense, they aren't much better than their 6-10 record indicates. The Chiefs' rushing leader in '85, Herman Heard, ranked seventeenth in the AFC with only 595 yards and a sorry 3.6-yards-per-carry average. Heralded rookie Ethan Horton averaged only 3.0 and may prove to be a major mistake. Ex-Brown Mike Pruitt may play a role again.

The quarterback picture is fairly clear. Bill Kenney, the AFC's fifth-ranked passer, can do the job when he isn't planted on his back. Backup Todd Blackledge finished the season strong, but he may not be the man of the future.

The offensive line must improve for the Chiefs to move up. Injuries hurt this group in '85, when Kaycee allowed 43 sacks. Brad Budde, John Alt, Matt Herkenhoff, and David Lutz all missed at least a month. G Rich Baldinger got good experience in Budde's place last year. C Bob Rush and top pick Brian Jozwiak should see plenty of action.

Defensively, a smooth season for ends Art Still and Mike Bell would certainly help. Despite their problems, they combined for 10 sacks in '85. Top sacker is NT Bill Mass. Dave Lindstrom and Eric Holle are ready to go at end and nose tackle, respectively.

Jerry Blanton can provide needed depth for Kaycee linebackers, if he's healthy. He joins with Scott Radecic, Calvin Daniels, Gary Spani, and Ken Jolly to form a decent quartet in 1986.

Deron Cherry, the starting safety for the AFC Pro Bowl team, is the leader of the Chiefs' secondary. Running mate Albert Lewis had eight interceptions, including six in his last three games. Lloyd Buruss and Kevin Ross are ready.

Where would the Chiefs have been without placekicker Nick Lowery? He hit on 24 of 27 FG attempts.

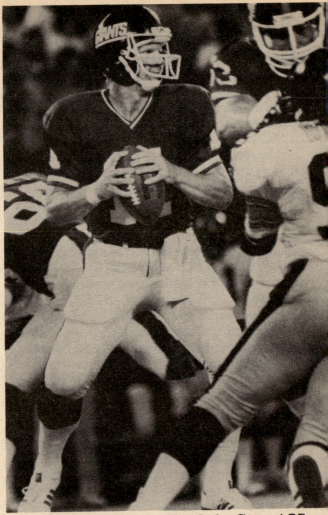

MVP of last year's Pro Bowl, the Giants' QB
Phil Simms has the NFL's second-best pass-
yardage total the last two years.

National Football Conference Team Previews

NFC East
NEW YORK GIANTS
1985 Finish: Second
1986 Prediction: First

Harry Carson   **Joe Morris**

Giant fans are so accustomed to losing, they cannot believe their team can win. True, the club hasn't won anything since 1963, and last year's home play-off game was the first since '62. No matter how strong a case you build for the team, old-line fans tell you that they'll figure out a way to lose.

Not this time. Off a season that included six losses by a *total* of only 20 points, the Giants might go all the way — maybe even to the Super Bowl!

QB Phil Simms has finally proven himself. The Pro Bowl MVP has thrown for 7,863 yards the last two seasons — second only to Dan Marino. RB Joe Morris, whose bulk, speed, and strength make up for his lack of height, set five team rushing records in '85, including most TDs (21) and most yards

(1,336). If backup George Adams conquers fumble-itis, the Giants will be set in this department. Rob Carpenter must be satisfied to be a blocker.

A healthy Lionel Manuel (49 catches, 859 yards despite missing four games) will strengthen the young receiving corps. Bobby Johnson (33 catches) and Phil McConkey (25) should return. TE Zeke Mowatt, one of the NFL's best, should be sound after a year's layoff (knee), rejoining tough Mark Bavaro.

C Bart Oates did a good job, along with improving Karl Nelson and vet Brad Benson at tackles and solid Billy Ard and Chris Godfrey at guard.

If All-Pro OLB Lawrence Taylor has his act together, the Giants' LBs should again be the NFC's best. There are no better than Taylor, Andy Headen, Byron Hunt, and Carl Banks on the outside with Gary Reasons and veteran Harry Carson on the inside. Up front, the Giants might look for another outstanding end to join sack king Leonard Marshall. Curtis McGriff, Casey Merrill, and George Martin are adequate, along with solid Jim Burt in the middle.

The defensive backs are in fair shape, even without the unhappy Mark Haynes (who was dealt to Denver). Elvis "Toast" Patterson led the club in interceptions, and Perry Williams, Terry Kinard, and Kenny Hill are good.

The return of Ali Haji-Sheikh will strengthen a so-so kicking game.

NFC East
WASHINGTON REDSKINS
1985 Finish: Third
1986 Prediction: Second

Dexter Manley   **Art Monk**

Broken leg or not, chances are that Joe Theismann would not have been the 'Skins' QB in '86. Whether Jay Schroeder is the answer remains to be seen.

Schroeder, who took over after Joe T.'s bone-crushing finale, led Washington to four wins in its last five outings. Babe Laufenberg will also contend for the position in training camp.

More depth is required at WR, where Art Monk (91 catches, best in the league) and Gary Clark (72 catches, fifth in the NFC) have matters well in hand.

The battle for No. 1 running back between George Rogers and John Riggins ended in a no-contest victory for Rogers (1,093 yards). Otis Wonsley and Keith Griffin will help in '86, with Kenny Jenkins a real possibility. Clint Didier proved to be a real find at TE (41 catches, 433 yards).

The offensive line is an especially bright spot, though there is a question about G R.C. Thielemann's health (knee). C Jeff Bostic appears totally fit again. Guards Ken Huff and All-Pro Russ Grimm and tackles Joe Jacoby and Mark May are standouts. Rick Donalley will be ready for full-time action soon.

Except for some needed depth at linebacker, the Washington defense is ready to go. If Bob Slater and Darryl Grant bounce back from their injuries, the line should be loaded. Ends Dexter Manley and Charles Mann are both coming off outstanding years ($29^1/_2$ sacks combined). Dean Hamel, who started at RT for Grant, will battle for the top spot again, with Dave Butz set at LT.

The LBs are beginning to age, but you can't tell off their '85 show. Mel Kaufman and Rich Milot on the outside and Neal Olkewicz in the middle each registered more than 100 tackles (Olkewicz had 174). Vet backup Monte Coleman has been hurt much of the time recently, and the 'Skins should be looking for youth here.

Despite a late-season slump, Washington ranked third in fewest TD passes allowed. There's plenty of youth here, with Raphel Cherry at SS and Barry Wilburn backing up both corners. CBs Darrell Green and Vernon Dean continue to go well, and FS Curtis Jordan is fine.

NFC East
DALLAS COWBOYS
1985 Finish: First
1986 Prediction: Third

Michael Downs   **Randy White**

If there's a way, Cowboy coach Tom Landry will find it. The man certainly knows
how to get his players to produce.

But as the '85 season came to a close, the
rust in the Cowboy armor began to show.
The 'Pokes lost three of the last four (50–24
to Cincinnati, 31–16 to San Francisco, and
20–0 to the Rams in the playoffs). They were
lucky to edge the Giants (28–21) to sew up
the division title. Trouble is, you never know
what Landry will do to recharge his forces.

There will, of course, be no quarterback
war in '86. Danny White won it in '85 with
10 TD passes (and only three interceptions)
in his last four games. Overall he threw for
2,157 yards and showed his clear leadership qualities once again.

RB Tony Dorsett remains at the top of his

game. His 1,307 yards ranked him fourth in the NFC and produced his eighth 1,000-yard season in his nine years. And he averaged 4.3 yards per carry. Not bad for an aging superstar. Trouble is, there's little talent behind him (unless the USFL folds and Herschel Walker moves to Dallas).

WR Tony Hill had another fine season (1,000-yards-plus for the third time, the first since 1980). TE Doug Cosbie should again be the NFC's best, averaging 12.4 yards per catch. WR Mike Renfro is underrated, and speedy Mike Sherrard of UCLA, the No. 1 draft, will match up well with Hill.

The offensive line is strong in the middle, with C Tom Rafferty and Gs Glen Titensor and Kurt Petersen. RT Jim Cooper bounced back from an injury, and Chris Schultz should again play LT ahead of Howard Richards.

The defensive line is probably better against the pass than the run. But only the Giants and Bears had more sacks in the NFC, and Jim Jeffcoat proved ready to join Randy White and Too Tall Jones up front.

Eugene Lockhart was up to the task at middle LB (for retired Bob Breunig), and vet Mike Hegman and young Jeff Rohrer are set on the outside. Steve DeOssie is a valuable backup.

NFL intercept leader (for the third time) Everson Walls and Dennis Thurman are highly regarded corners. Dextor Clinckscale and Michael Downs should again be at safety.

NFC East
PHILADELPHIA EAGLES
1985 Finish: Fourth
1986 Prediction: Fourth

Mike Quick   **Earnest Jackson**

If the Eagles can get off to a decent start (they lost four of the first five in '85), they'll make a genius out of new coach Buddy Ryan. The mastermind of the Super Bears' 46 defense, Ryan gets his first shot at an NFL head coaching job. Unfortunately, he doesn't have the athletes who did so well for him in Chicago.

There are problems at quarterback. Vet Ron Jaworski bounced back from an early-season benching to lead Philly back into the NFC East race. But he served up 17 interceptions in his last eight games (only nine TDs). Backup Randall Cunningham is a great runner, fair thrower.

Ex-Charger Earnest Jackson became the first NFL player with consecutive 1,000-yard seasons in two different uniforms. He picked up 1,028 yards on 282 carries. A healthy Keith Byars — a first-round draft gamble — would really help.

The receiving corps is excellent. Mike Quick, No. 4 in the NFC and an easy Pro Bowl choice, caught 73 for 1,247 yards (17.1 average). Running mate Kenny Jackson averaged 17.3 yards per catch. TE John Spagnola is reliable (64 receptions and five TDs).

Coach Ryan will closely monitor the offensive line that turned things around after a terrible first month in '85. LT Ken Reeves was a pleasant rookie surprise, along with C Mark Dennard. RT Leonard Mitchell is a fine blocker. Guards Steve Kenney and Ron Baker are okay.

Ryan has plenty of talent on the defensive line. DLE Reggie White was a real find after coming over from the USFL. DRE Greg Brown was the club sack leader (13). They're a fine pair. In the middle, Ken Clarke does a good job. But it's hard to tell what Ryan will do with this group.

Among the LBs, ex-Lion Garry Cobb was a fine pickup at ROLB. LILB Mike Reichenbach is coming off a fine season. RILB Anthony Griggs is a pro. Watch for big changes here.

The new coaching staff should be pleased with All-Pro FS Wes Hopkins, a superstar when he's healthy. SS Ray Ellis is a fine partner for Hopkins. CBs Roynell Young and Elbert Foules will join with aging (but still excellent) Herman Edwards.

NFC East
ST. LOUIS CARDINALS
1985 Finish: Fifth
1986 Predictions: Fifth

Stump Mitchell   **E.J. Junior**

The most interesting announcement of the off-season? St. Louis promised that 3,000 seats would be added to Busch Stadium. Exactly what the football Cards need: 3,000 more empty seats.

The Cardinals' pitiful performance in '85 chased the fans from the stands and Jim Hanifan from the coaching lines. The people are there to turn things around, but it's unlikely to happen in the tough NFC East. Only a reduced-quality schedule provides any real hope.

QB Neil Lomax, one of the NFL's best in '84 (4,614 yards), slumped to only 3,214 yards in '85. Arm and shoulder miseries plus a porous offensive line contributed to his difficulties. Backup Scott Brunner is fair.

If Ottis (O.J.) Anderson bounces back

from his knee and ankle problems, the Cards' running game could bounce back. Not that Stump Mitchell (1,006 yards, 5.5 yards per carry) can't do the job. He just can't do it by himself.

Though Roy Green, one of the league's top WRs, wasn't 100 percent in '85, he showed that he can do it in all circumstances. He caught 50 passes for 693 yards, with running mate Pat Tilley getting 726 yards on 49 receptions. J.T. Smith is a valuable backup. TE Doug Marsh (37 for 355 yards) is good.

On the line, LT Luis Sharpe wasn't (sharp, that is), on his return from the USFL. The line allowed 65 sacks, the most in Card history. Tootie Robbins may win his RT job back from Lance Smith. Guards Joe Bostic and Doug Dawson and center Randy Clark should start again.

Defensively, the Cards' sack total dropped nearly in half from '84, and they allowed 20 more yards rushing per game in '85. Ugh! DLT Mark Duda played well. But DLE Bubba Baker slumped badly, and DRE Curtis Greer and DLT David Galloway were just so-so.

The linebackers are a bit better. MLB E.J. Junior is first-rate (and a Pro Bowler). LLB Niko Noga is a comer, and RLB Freddie Joe Nunn has a great future. So does top draft pick Anthony Bell of Michigan State.

The secondary is something else. They allowed 34 TD passes in '85, which was tops in the league. Major changes are in store.

NFC Central
CHICAGO BEARS
1985 Finish: First
1986 Prediction: First

Dan Hampton　　　　　　　　　　**Otis Wilson**

Here's the word on the Chicago Bears:
"The Bears are a perfectly balanced football team. They're primed with experience
and talent. They have great coaching and
great players. They're one of the greatest
teams in the history of the game."

Whose words are those? Not ours, though
we wrote last year that "the Bears have the
best talent in the league." Not coach Mike
Ditka's, though he probably believes them.

No, that analysis comes from New England Patriot coach Raymond Berry and
was uttered just after Chicago's 46–10
smashing of his Pats in Super Bowl XX.

There isn't a reason to believe that the
Bears won't be representing the NFC again
come Super Bowl XXI in Pasadena in January. Chicago is still loaded for, er, Bear,

though the road to California could be a little trickier than last year's trek.

How much will Chicago miss defensive boss Buddy Ryan, the Eagles' new head coach? Buddy took his famed 46 defense with him, and the Bears will likely change schemes this time around. But the talent is still there, with Pro Bowl starters MLB Mike Singletary and DRE Richard Dent, along with backups LLB Otis Wilson, DLE Dan Hampton, and SS Dave Duerson. Tackles Steve McMichael and Fridge Perry should be even better. The rest of the defense is set, with injured Leslie Frazier the only question mark.

The continued success of flaky QB Jim McMahon (178 completions, 2,392 yards, 15 TDs) will always raise questions. But all-timer RB Walter "Sweetness" Payton (1,551 yards rushing, 483 yards receiving) can usually carry the whole club. Matt Suhey (471 yards) is the perfect partner.

You couldn't tell on Super Sunday, but the receivers are probably the Bears' weakest link. Payton was the top catcher, and though Willie Gault tied for the best per-catch yardage in the NFL, he had only one TD. Chicago needs a possession receiver.

The line, led by All-Pros like C Jay Hilgenberg and LT Jim Covert, is underrated. RT Keith Van Horne is first-rate, and guards Tom Thayer and Mark Bortz give 100 percent all the time.

Super again? Why not?

NFC Central
DETROIT LIONS
1985 Finish: Third (tied)
1986 Prediction: Second

Leonard Thompson   **Eric Hipple**

Talk about Dr. Jekyll and Mr. Hyde. The Lions were monsters at home in '85, winning their first six at the Silverdome and finishing 6–2. Meanwhile, they were perfect gentlemen on the road, losing their last seven away games after a one-point victory in the opener. The result was a much improved 7–9 record — with miles to go.

QB Eric Hipple was the author of the modern Jekyll-Hyde tale. An All-Pro at home (13 TD passes during the win streak), he was absolutely awful on the road (no TDs during the seven straight losses). Credit home cooking or the dome roof, Hipple must develop consistency. Top pick Chuck Long of Iowa may heat up soon.

RB James Jones proved up to the task when Billy Sims was lost. Jones wound up with 886 yards rushing (and another 334 receiving). Ex-Eagle Wilbert Montgomery still has enough left to be a solid backup.

In-and-out WR Leonard Thompson was in most of the time (including three TDs vs. the Jets). Mark Nichols, Jeff Chadwick, and Carl Bland are excellent partners. TE David Lewis can do more.

Up front, Chris Dieterich will join ex-tackle Keith Dorney at guard, with future star Lomas Brown and Rich Strenger at tackle. Steve Mott will battle Kevin Glover at center.

Defensively, the Lions will have to find a way to stop opposing runners. When your safeties are your team's leading tacklers, you know you have troubles up front. Another year's experience with the 3–4 defense may help, as will the return of Doug English. NT Curtis Green and ends William Gay and Keith Ferguson could improve. Eric Williams should play more.

If last year's wounded are healthy, the linebacking corps could be solid. LOLB Jimmy Williams is a fine tackler and pass-rusher, with Kurt Allerman at RILB, August Curley at LILB, and Mike Cofer at ROLB. Roosevelt Barnes, James Harrell, and Angelo King are on the comeback trail.

Despite allowing only 16 TD passes, the Lions' secondary is questionable. Safeties Demetrious Johnson, William Frizzell, and William Graham are sound tacklers. Corners Bruce McNorton and Bobby Watkins are okay.

NFC Central
GREEN BAY PACKERS
1985 Finish: Second
1986 Prediction: Third

James Lofton   **Mike Douglass**

Just a few seasons back, the Packers were the NFL's worst defensive team. Coach Forrest Gregg has changed all that and brought respectability to the Green Bay defense. Now it's the offense that needs strengthening, particularly in the backfield. Still, no one in the NFC Central is catching up with the Super Bowl champion Bears for at least a couple of seasons. The Pack is thus advised to build slowly and carefully.

Defensively, ends Ezra Johnson and Alphonso Carreker combined for 18½ sacks a year ago, a decent enough performance. NT Donnie Humphrey does extremely well when he's healthy.

The Pack's top '85 rookie, Brian Noble, was a pleasant surprise at RILB. He joined with Randy Scott inside and John Anderson outside. Veteran Mike Douglass continued to do an outstanding job.

Green Bay could use a hand or two in the defensive backfield where RCB Tim Lewis was the top interceptor (four). Barring a deal, the Packers, who did not have a first-round draft pick, will probably go with Mark Lee on the other corner and Mark Murphy and Tom Flynn at the safeties. It would help if expensive Mossy Cade played up to potential.

Lynn Dickey (172 completions, 15 TDs) is probably still the best of the Green Bay QBs, but he has been banged around badly. Much-traveled Vince Ferragamo will get a long look in training camp, because Randy Wright and Jim Zorn probably aren't up to the task. To his credit, Wright did play well in relief of Dickey last season.

Look for Gary Ellerson to see more action at RB after playing well in the last stages of '85. The veteran trio, Eddie Lee Ivery (636 yards), Jessie Clark (633), and Gerry Ellis (571), do fairly well.

The Pack has outstanding receivers, led by one of the game's best, James Lofton (69 catches, 1,153 yards). Speedy Phillip Epps (44 catches) and TE Paul Coffman (49 receptions for 666 yards) round out the standout trio.

The kicking game is in able hands (and feet). PK Al Del Greco won four games with field goals, and P Don Bracken (40.5-yard average) could keep the job for a while.

NFC Central
MINNESOTA VIKINGS
1985 Finish: Third (tied)
1986 Prediction: Fourth

Tommy Kramer   **Anthony Carter**

After 20 years of waiting in the wings as
an NFL assistant coach, Jerry Burns finally
gets his chance to be head coach. Given his
choice, he probably would have picked a
different team. But the one-year return of
Bud Grant did help the team start back on
the road to the top.

Burns, who knows a thing or three about
offense, inherits a mixed bag from his old
boss. Minny finished third in the NFC in
passing, despite QB Tommy Kramer's low-
est rating ever (67.8, eleventh in the NFC).
Kramer simply threw the ball more than
anyone else and wound up with 3,522 yards
and 19 TDs (but also 26 interceptions).

Kramer's performance should improve,
thanks to the wonderful ability of Anthony
Carter (43 catches, 821 yards, 8 TDs), who

could become one of the NFL's best. TE Steve Jordan (68 receptions) is a good possession receiver. Mike Jones is fine.

It's the running game that really warrants Burns's attention (and, hopefully, a new big back). Darrin Nelson came off the scrap heap to gain 893 yards on 200 carries a year ago; while '84's ace, Alfred Anderson, carried only 50 times for 121 yards. Veteran Ted Brown still has a few yards left in him.

The offensive line is much improved, with tackles David Huffman and Tim Irwin and guards Brent Boyd and Terry Tausch. Look for Dennis Swilley and Kirk Lowdermilk to battle for the center spot in '86. A big offensive lineman would help, too.

There are plenty of questions on defense, starting with DE Neil Elshire's health. DE Keith Millard is great against the pass, not so great against the run. NT Tim Newton should improve.

Grant cleaned house at the linebacker spots last year, slicing a couple of former All-Pros. Vet Scott Studwell should be well enough to start on the inside in '86, along with David Howard. Top '85 draftee Chris Doleman should return on the outside. Top '86 pick Gerald Robinson may start.

The backfield was the most improved a year ago, doubling their previous interception total. SS Joey Browner is great against the run, and FS John Turner led the club in pickoffs. Carl Lee and Willie Teal should again man the corners.

NFC Central
TAMPA BAY BUCCANEERS
1985 Finish: Fifth
1986 Prediction: Fifth

Kevin House   **James Wilder**

The Bucs' first coach, John McKay, arrived from Southern Cal as a coaching legend. He didn't win much, but he stayed as long as he wanted, then left as a legend. His successor, current boss Leeman Bennett, doesn't enjoy McKay's status. Another 2–14 season would send the one-time Falcon boss to the unemployment line again.

It could happen. Chances are he'll open the '86 season with ex-USFLer Steve Young, who replaced Steve DeBerg at quarterback late last year. Young is mobile and can make the big play. But his major advantage over DeBerg is that he lost only four games last year to DeBerg's ten.

Buc (and NFL fans) spent the spring arguing whether Tampa should draft Auburn's superback Bo Jackson. The Jackson people pointed out that a great back like Bo comes along rarely. The anti-Jacksons said that James Wilder, hard-working and productive (1,300 yards on 365 tough carries), can do the job. The top draft pick, they reasoned, could best be spent elsewhere.

TE Jimmie Giles needs a full season like the first half of 1985. He had only 12 receptions in the last six games, allowing Kevin House (44 catches, 803 yards) to lead the receivers. RB Wilder, however, was the Buc leader with 53 catches.

The offensive line can be awful (21 sacks in Young's five starts) or wonderful (none against the Bears). Injuries, of course, played a role. Still, RG Sean Farrell continues to shine, and C Randy Grimes and RT Randy Heller are excellent.

With Lee Roy Selmon now retired, the defensive line will struggle again. DRE Ron Holmes should continue to grow. DLE John Cannon must return to his old form. NT Dave Logan is fine against the pass.

LOLB Ervin Randle had a fine rookie year, replacing departed Hugh Green. ILBs Scot Brantley and Jeff Davis are especially good against the run.

A decent performance late in the season gives promise for the Buc secondary. LCB Jeremiah Castille is a top ball-thief, and ex-Ram FS Ivory Sully is fine on run coverage. David Greenwood and Craig Curry will battle for the SS starting spot, with John Holt likely again at RCB.

NFC West
SAN FRANCISCO 49ERS
1985 Finish: Second
1986 Prediction: First

Michael Carter   **Roger Craig**

Coach Bill Walsh hopes for a more consistent season for his 'Niners in '86. That would return San Francisco to the top of the NFC West, where, of course, he believes, they belong.

So do we. John Robinson did one of the finest coaching jobs in coaxing the Rams to the division title last year. But the elimination of a few key 49er turnovers and improved health by important regulars should reverse the results in '86.

The Niners discovered a new superstar last year in RB Roger Craig. He became the first NFL player ever to gain 1,000 yards both rushing and receiving. QB Joe Montana continues among the NFL's top signal-callers, tossing 27 TD passes among his 303 completions for 3,653 yards. He had only

13 interceptions, but most came in big spots in 49er losses. The health of runners Wendell Tyler (867 yards) and Derrick Harmon is vital.

The receiving corps is outstanding. WR Dwight Clark (54 catches) led the club with 10 TDs. Speedy rookie Jerry Rice caught 49 passes for an 18.9 average. And aging TE Russ Francis had his best year (44 receptions, 478 yards).

An injury-riddled offensive line allowed more sacks than usual. Former All-Pro Keith Fahnhorst remains a major force along with fellow tackle Bubba Paris. The return of G Randy Cross will help. He'll match up with John Ayers, with Guy McIntyre ready to step in. C Fred Quillan is among the NFL's best.

The defense is first-rate. NT Michael Carter should be a Pro Bowl regular with DE John Harty ready to become a starter with Dwaine Board. DEs Jeff Stover and Fred Dean are fine in passing situations, but Dean is now 34 and in need of help.

Linebacking is in fine hands, with Keena Turner and Todd Shell on the outside and Riki Ellison and Michael Walter on the inside. There's decent depth, too, though more is expected of Turner than he showed in '85.

The secondary features all past and present Pro Bowlers. Top interceptor (with six) Ronnie Lott is now set at FS, though he prefers to play the corner. CB Eric Wright and SS Carlton Williamson are among the league's best.

NFC West
LOS ANGELES RAMS
1985 Finish: First
1986 Prediction: Second

Eric Dickerson   **Kent Hill**

If we were starting a new NFL club, we'd probably make whatever deal it would take to get John Robinson as our coach. The Rams' bossman has done a marvelous job, winning the NFC West and reaching the NFC finals last year, despite personnel that didn't match up to the 'Niners and Bears.

The Rams have some great strengths, particularly with Eric Dickerson (1,234 yards rushing and 12 TDs), the running marvel who missed the first two weeks of '85 in a contract squabble. He also beat Dallas in the play-offs with 248 ground yards.

The offensive line features a quartet of Pro Bowlers, with center Doug Smith, guards Kent Hill and Dennis Harrah, and tackle Jackie Slater. The one non-Bowler, tackle Irv Pankey, isn't too shabby.

A healthy Ron Brown will key an improvement in the wide receiver corps. Henry Ellard (54 catches, 811 yards) does well, and TE Tony Hunter, the ex-Bill, had his best year ever (50 receptions, 562 yards).

Quarterback remains the major question. Dieter Brock, the former Canadian star, threw for only 2,658 yards, but he kept the ball moving and threw only 13 interceptions. Jeff Kemp is gone. Free agent Steve Bartkowski should challenge Brock.

The defensive line should continue to show improvement. There's strength at the nose with Charlie DeJurnett and young Shawn Miller. The three top ends, Doug Reed, Reggie Doss, and ex-Giant Gary Jeter, do a strong job. Jeter was the sack leader.

The linebacking crew, likewise, is improved. RILB Jim Collins is proving deadly against the run, and LOLB Mel Owens is really beginning to sparkle. Mike Wilcher on the right outside and Carl Ekern on the left inside are probably underrated.

Left corner Gary Green is again playing up to his former All-Pro standards (reached with Kansas City). A healthy Nolan Cromwell at strong safety and Johnnie Johnson at free safety make a powerful difference in this group. Pro Bowler Leroy Irvin is a stick-out at the right corner.

The kicking game is in excellent shape. P Dale Hatcher averaged 43.2-yards in his rookie year. Vet PK Mike Lansford hit on 22 of 29 FG tries.

NFC West
NEW ORLEANS SAINTS
1985 Finish: Third
1986 Prediction: Third

Bobby Hebert   **Rickey Jackson**

Chances are new coach Jim Mora will quickly learn that his Saints bear little resemblance to his former team, the USFL champion Baltimore Stars. Former coaches Bum and Wade Phillips left the club ripe for another rebuilding plan. Mora will need more building blocks than he has.

USFL star Bobby Hebert should be the top QB this time around. Last year's starter, Dave Wilson, and backup Richard Todd couldn't do the job. Hebert played fairly well late in the season and deserves a full shot. His rating for his brief '85 appearance would have placed him within the first half-dozen NFC passers.

Whether Earl Campbell has another big season in him is questionable. The one-time Oiler superstar finished well in '85 and wound up with 642 yards rushing. Wayne Wilson (645 yards) was the Saints' top rusher in '85, but a healthy Hokie Gajan might have outstripped them all. A quick outside runner would really help.

The receiving group leaves much to be desired. TE Hoby Brenner (42 catches, 652 yards) is solid. But Eugene Goodlow (32 for 603) isn't good enough, and Lindsay Scott may be a bust. Eric Martin is a decent backup man.

The offensive line showed some improvement, notably from LG Brad Edelman, C Steve Korte, and RT Stan Brock. Top pick Jim Dombrowski of Virginia should start in '86.

If LE Bruce Clark returns to form and NT Derland Moore returns to health, the Saints' defensive line should improve. Look for defensive ends Frank Warren and James Geathers to get more playing time.

One big Mora project is LOLB Rickey Jackson, who did well on the field but carried on a war with ex-coach Bum Phillips. RILB Jack Del Rio was fine in his first year out of Southern Cal. ROLB James Haynes should continue to improve, and better play from ILB Alvin Toles would help. The return of Jim Kovach is important.

The secondary is decent, with FS Frank Wattelet a fine tackler and LCB Dave Waymer a good ball-hawk. SS Terry Hoage and RCB Johnnie Poe should be back.

Placekicker Morten Anderson and punter Brian Hansen provide strong kicking.

NFL West
ATLANTA FALCONS
1985 Finish: Fourth
1986 Prediction: Fourth

Gerald Riggs   **Bobby Butler**

About the safest prediction for the Falcons '86 season is that coach Dan Henning is most likely to be the first coach fired — if the Falcons don't win early. Not that Henning isn't a terrific guy or that he doesn't have his players playing hard. It's just that Atlanta was 8–24 the past two years under his leadership, and that simply isn't good enough.

If Henning doesn't find a pro quarterback somewhere, winning will be downright impossible. Bruised and beaten Steve Bartkowski, who was Atlanta's main man for many years, is gone. His replacement, David Archer, ranked fourteenth among NFC passers in '85. In his defense, he's a lot more mobile than Bart. But that isn't the first thing you look for in an NFL QB. Ex-

Bengal Turk Schonert could be just what the Falcons need.

The running game, on the other hand, is in much better shape. Gerald Riggs was a pleasant surprise, finishing first in the NFC and second in the NFL with 1,719 yards and eight 100-yard-plus games (though Atlanta was 1–7 in those games). Ex-Redskin Joe Washington should fill in again.

Having a healthy Charlie Brown all season should help the receivers. TE Arthur Cox is first-rate as blocker and receiver. White Shoes Johnson has bounced back to be a solid force.

If Ts Mike Kenn and Brett Miller and G John Scully all return to good health, the offensive line might be decent. Future All-Pro G-T Bill Fralic is the best Atlanta has, with Jeff Kiewel and Joe Pellegrini just so-so at G and Wayne Radloff still a big "if" at C.

The defensive line is fair, especially ends Rick Bryan and Mike Pitts and tackle Dan Benish. NT Tony Casillas, the second pick overall in the draft, will become a star. Linebacking is spotty, especially in rushing the passer. Brainy first-rounder Tim Green of Syracuse should help.

James Britt and Kenny Johnson should return from injuries to strengthen the secondary. Wendell Cason and Tiger Greene will likely return to the bench. Bobby Butler and Scott Case are okay.

PK Mick Luckhurst is a folk hero in Atlanta — a success in a sea of failure.

1986 NFL Draft List

The following abbreviations are used to identify the players' positions:

OFFENSE: T = tackle;   G = guard;
C = center;   QB = quarterback;
RB = running back; WR = wide receiver;
TE = tight end.

DEFENSE: DE = defensive end;
DT = defensive tackle;   LB = linebacker;
DB = defensive back.

SPECIAL TEAMS: P = punter;
K = placekicker;   KR = kick returner.

The number preceding the player's name indicates the round during which he was drafted. A letter following the number indicates that the team had more than one choice in that round.

Atlanta Falcons

1. Tony Casillas, DT, Oklahoma; 1a. Tim Green, LB, Syracuse; 6. Floyd Dixon, WR, Stephen F. Austin; 6a. Keith Williams, RB, S.W. Missouri; 8. Kevin Hudgens, DE, Idaho State; 9. Kevin Starks, TE, Minnesota; 10. Tony Baker, RB, East Carolina; 11. Chris Hegg, QB, N.E. Missouri; 12. Steve Griffin, WR, Purdue.

Buffalo Bills

1. Ronnie Harmon, RB, Iowa; 1a. Will Wolford, T, Vanderbilt; 3. Leonard Burton, C, South Carolina; 5. Carl Byrum, RB, Mississippi Valley; 7. Bob Williams, TE, Penn State; 7a. Mark Pike, DT, Georgia Tech; 7b. Butch Rolle, TE, Michigan State; 8. Tony Furjanic, LB, Notre Dame; 9. Reggie Bynum, WR, Oregon State; 10. Guy Teafatiller, DT, Illinois; 11. Tony Garbarczyk, DT, Wake Forest; 11a. Billy Witt, DE, North Alabama; 12. Brian McClure, QB, Bowling Green; 12a. Derek Christian, LB, West Virginia.

Chicago Bears

1. Neal Anderson, RB, Florida; 2. Vestee Jackson, DB, Washington; 3. David Williams, WR, Illinois; 4. Paul Blair, T, Oklahoma State; 5. Lew Barnes, WR, Oregon; 6. Jeff Powell, RB, Tennessee; 7. Bruce Jones, DB, North Alabama; 8. Maurice Douglass, DB, Kentucky; 9. John Teltschik, P, Texas; 10. Barton Hundley, DB, Kansas State; 11. Glen Kozlowski, WR, Brigham Young.

Cincinnati Bengals

1. Joe Kelly, LB, Washington; 1a. Tim McGee, WR, Tennessee; 2. Lewis Billups, DB, North Alabama; 3. Jim Skow, DE, Nebraska; 3a. Mike Hammerstein, DT, Michigan; 3b. David Fulcher, DB, Arizona State; 4. Eric Kattus, TE, Michigan; 4a. Doug Gaynor, QB, Cal State-Long Beach; 5. Leon White, LB, Brigham Young; 6. Gary Hunt, DB, Memphis State; 7. Pat Franklin, RB, S.W. Texas State; 8. David Douglas, G, Tennessee; 9. Cary Whittingham, LB, Brigham Young; 10. Jeff Shaw, DT, Salem, W. Va.; 11. Tim Stone, T, Kansas State; 11a. Tom Flaherty, LB, Northwestern; 12. Steve Bradley, QB, Indiana.

Cleveland Browns

2. Webster Slaughter, WR, San Diego State; 5. Nick Miller, LB, Arkansas; 7. Jim Meyer, T, Illinois State; 7a. Mike Norseth, QB, Kansas; 9. Danny Taylor, DB, Texas-El Paso; 10. Willie Smith, TE, Miami; 11. Randy

Dausin, G, Texas A&M; 12. King Simmons, DB, Texas Tech.

Dallas Cowboys

1. Mike Sherrard, WR, UCLA; 2. Darryl Clack, RB, Arizona State; 3. Mark Walen, DT, UCLA; 4. Max Zendejas, K, Arizona; 6. Thornton Chandler, TE, Alabama; 6a. Stan Gelbaugh, QB, Maryland; 6b. Lloyd Yancey, G, Temple; 7. Johnny Holloway, WR, Kansas; 8. Topper Clemons, RB, Wake Forest; 9. John Ionata, G, Florida State; 10. Bryan Chester, G, Texas; 11. Garth Jax, LB, Florida State; 12. Chris Duliban, LB, Texas; 12a. Tony Flack, DB, Georgia.

Denver Broncos

4. Jim Juriga, T, Illinois; 5. Tony Colorito, DT, Southern California; 6. Orson Mobley, TE, Salem, W. Va.; 6a. Mark Jackson, WR, Purdue; 7. Raymond Phillips, LB, North Carolina State; 8. Bruce Klostermann, LB, South Dakota State; 9. Joe Thomas, WR, Mississippi Valley; 10. Victor Hall, TE, Jackson State; 11. Thomas Dendy, RB, South Carolina.

Detroit Lions

1. Chuck Long, QB, Iowa; 2. Garry James, RB, Louisiana State; 3. Joe Milinichik, T, North Carolina State; 4. Devon Mitchell, DB, Iowa; 5. Oscar Smith, RB, Nicholls State; 8. Allyn Griffin, WR, Wyoming; 9. Lyle Pickens, DB, Colorado; 10. Tracy Johnson, LB, Morningside; 11. Leland Melvin, WR, Richmond; 12. Allan Durden, DB, Arizona.

Green Bay Packers

2. Kenneth Davis, RB, Texas Christian; 3. Robbie Bosco, QB, Brigham Young; 4. Tim Harris, LB, Memphis State; 4a. Dan Knight, T, San Diego State; 5. Matt Koart, DT, Southern California; 6. Burnell Dent, LB, Tulane; 7. Ed Berry, DB, Utah State; 8. Michael Cline, DT, Arkansas State; 9. Brent Moore, DT, Southern California; 10. Gary Spann, LB, Texas Christian.

Houston Oilers

1. Jim Everett, QB, Purdue; 2. Ernest Givins, WR, Louisville; 3. Allen Pinkett, RB, Notre Dame; 5. Jeff Parks, TE, Auburn; 6. Ray Wallace, RB, Purdue; 8. Larry Griffin, DB, North Carolina; 9. Bob Sebring, LB, Illinois; 10. Don Sommer, G, Texas-El Paso; 11. Mark Cochran, T, Baylor; 12. Chuck Banks, RB, West Virginia Tech.

Indianapolis Colts

1. Jon Hand, DE, Alabama; 2. Jack Trudeau, QB, Illinois; 4. Bill Brooks, WR, Boston U.; 5. Scott Kellar, DE, Northern Illinois; 5a. Gary Walker, C, Boston U.; 7. Steve O'Malley, DT, Northern Illinois; 7a. Chris White, K, Illinois; 7b. Tommy Sims, DB, Tennessee; 8. Trell Hooper, DB, Memphis State; 9. Bob Brotzki, T, Syracuse; 10. Pete Anderson, G, Georgia; 12. Steve Wade, DT, Vanderbilt; 12a. Isaac Williams, DT, Florida State.

Kansas City Chiefs

1. Brian Jozwiak, T, West Virginia; 2. Dino Hackett, LB, Appalachian State; 3. Leonard Griffin, DE, Grambling; 4. Tom Baugh, C, Southern Illinois; 4a. Chas Fox, WR, Furman; 6. Kent Hagood, RB, South Carolina; 8. Lewis Colbert, P, Auburn; 9. Gary Baldinger, DE, Wake Forest; 10. Ike Readon, DT, Hampton; 11. Aaron Pearson, LB, Mississippi State.

Los Angeles Raiders

1. Bob Buczkowski, DE, Pittsburgh; 3. Brad Cochran, DB, Michigan; 4. Mike Wise, DE, Cal-Davis; 4a. Vance Mueller, RB, Occidental; 4b. Napoleon McCallum, RB, Navy; 6. Doug Marrone, T, Syracuse; 7. Bill Lewis, C, Nebraska; 8. Joe Mauntel, LB, Eastern Kentucky; 9. Zeph Lee, RB, Southern California; 10. Jeff Reinke, DE, Mankato State; 11. Randell Webster, LB, S.W. Oklahoma; 12. Larry Shepherd, WR, Houston.

Los Angeles Rams

1. Mike Schad, T, Queen's U., Can.; 2. Tom Newberry, G, LaCrosse, Wis.; 3. Hugh Millen, QB, Washington; 6. Robert Cox, T, UCLA; 6a. Lynn Williams, RB, Kan-

sas; 8. Steve Jarecki, LB, UCLA; 8a. Hank Goebel, T, Cal State-Fullerton; 9. Elbert Watts, DB, Southern California; 10. Garrett Breeland, LB, Southern California; 11. Chul Schwanke, RB, South Dakota; 12. Marcus Dupree, RB, Oklahoma.

Miami Dolphins

2. John Offerdahl, LB, Western Michigan; 3. T.J. Turner, DT, Houston; 4. James Pruitt, WR, Cal State-Fullerton; 5. Kevin Wyatt, DB, Arkansas; 6. Brent Sowell, DT, Alabama; 7. Larry Kolic, LB, Ohio State; 8. John Stuart, T, Texas; 9. Reyna Thompson, DB, Baylor; 10. Jeff Wickersham, QB, Louisiana State; 11. Arnold Franklin, TE, North Carolina; 12. Rickey Isom, RB, North Carolina State.

Minnesota Vikings

1. Gerald Robinson, DE, Auburn; 4. Joe Phillips, DT, Southern Methodist; 5. Hassan Jones, WR, Florida State; 6. Thomas Rooks, RB, Illinois; 7. Carl Hilton, TE, Houston; 8. Gary Schippang, T, West Chester, Pa.; 9. Mike Slaton, DB, South Dakota; 10. Joe Cormier, WR, Southern California; 11. John Armstrong, DB, Richmond; 12. Jesse Solomon, LB, Florida State.

New England Patriots

1. Reggie Dupard, RB, Southern Methodist; 2. Mike Ruth, DT, Boston College; 2a. Vencie Glenn, DB, Indiana State; 4. Scott Gieselman, TE, Boston College; 5. Greg Robinson, G, Cal State-Sacramento; 7. Ray McDonald, WR, Florida; 7a. Brent Williams, DE, Toledo; 8. Greg Baty, TE, Stanford; 9. George Colton, G, Maryland; 10. Cletis Jones, RB, Florida State; 11. Gene Thomas, WR, Pacific; 12. Don McAulay, K, Syracuse.

New Orleans Saints

1. Jim Dombrowski, T, Virginia; 2. Dalton Hilliard, RB, Louisiana State; 3. Rueben Mayes, RB, Washington State; 3a. Pat Swilling, LB, Georgia Tech; 3b. Barry Word, RB, Virginia; 4. Kelvin Edwards, WR, Liberty Baptist; 5. Reggie Sutton, DB, Miami; 6. Robert

Thompson, WR, Youngstown; 7. Gill Fenerty, RB, Holy Cross; 8. Filipo Mokofisi, LB, Utah; 9. Merlon Jones, LB, Florida A&M; 10. Jon Dumbauld, DE, Kentucky; 11. Pat Swoopes, DT, Mississippi State; 12. Sebastian Brown, WR, Bethune-Cookman.

New York Giants

1. Eric Dorsey, DE, Notre Dame; 2. Mark Collins, DB, Cal State-Fullerton; 2a. Erik Howard, DT, Washington State; 2b. Pepper Johnson, LB, Ohio State; 2c. Greg Lasker, DB, Arkansas; 3. John Washington, DE, Oklahoma State; 5. Vince Warren, WR, San Diego State; 6. Ron Brown, WR, Colorado; 6a. Solomon Miller, WR, Utah State; 7. Jon Francis, RB, Boise State; 8. Steve Cisowski, T, Santa Clara; 9. Jim Luebbers, DE, Iowa State; 10. Jerry Kimmel, LB, Syracuse; 11. Len Lynch, G, Maryland.

New York Jets

1. Mike Haight, T, Iowa; 2. Doug Williams, T, Texas A&M; 3. Tim Crawford, LB, Texas Tech; 4. Rogers Alexander, LB, Penn State; 5. Ron Hadley, LB, Washington; 7. Bob White, T, Rhode Island; 8. Robert Ducksworth, DB, So. Mississippi; 9. Nuu Faaola, RB, Hawaii; 10. Carl Carr, LB, North Carolina; 11. Vince Amoia, RB, Arizona State; 12. Sal Cesario, T, Cal Poly-Obispo.

Philadelphia Eagles

1. Keith Byars, RB, Ohio State; 2. Anthony Toney, RB, Texas A&M; 2a. Alonzo Johnson, LB, Florida; 4. Matt Darwin, C, Texas A&M; 5. Ray Criswell, P, Florida; 5a. Dan McMillen, DE, Colorado; 6. Bob Landsee, C, Wisconsin; 7. Corn Redick, WR, Cal State-Fullerton; 7a. Byron Lee, LB, Ohio State; 8. Seth Joyner, LB, Texas-El Paso; 9. Clyde Simmons, DE, Western Carolina; 10. Junior Tautalatasi, RB, Washington State; 11. Steve Bogdalek, G, Michigan State; 12. Reggie Singletary, DE, North Carolina State; 12a. Bobby Howard, RB, Indiana.

Pittsburgh Steelers

1. John Rienstra, G, Temple; 2. Gerald Williams, DE, Auburn; 3. Walter Brister, QB, N.E. Louisiana; 4. Bill Callahan, DB, Pittsburgh; 5. Erroll Tucker, DB, Utah; 5a. Brent Jones, TE, Santa Clara; 6. Domingo Bryant, DB, Texas A&M; 7. Rodney Carter, RB, Purdue; 8. Cap Boso, TE, Illinois; 9. Anthony Henton, LB, Troy State; 10. Warren Seitz, WR, Missouri; 11. Larry Station, LB, Iowa; 12. Mike Williams, LB, Tulsa.

St. Louis Cardinals

1. Anthony Bell, LB, Michigan State; 2. John Lee, K, UCLA; 3. Gene Chilton, C, Texas; 4. Carl Carter, DB, Texas Tech; 5. Jeff Tupper, DE, Oklahoma; 7. Eric Swanson, WR, Tennessee; 8. Ray Brown, G, Arkansas State; 9. Kent Kafentzis, DB, Hawaii; 10. Vai Sikahema, RB, Brigham Young; 10a. Wes Smith, WR, East Texas State; 11. Wayne Dillard, LB, Alcorn State; 12. Kent Austin, QB, Mississippi.

San Diego Chargers

1. Leslie O'Neal, DE, Oklahoma State; 1a. James Fitzpatrick, T, Southern California; 3. Terry Unrein, DE, Colorado State; 3a. Jeff Walker, T, Memphis State; 4. Ty Allert, LB, Texas; 4a. Tommy Taylor, LB, UCLA; 5. Doug Landry, LB, Louisiana Tech; 5a. Donald Brown, DB, Maryland; 5b. Matt Johnson, DB, Southern California; 6. Curt Pardridge, WR, Northern Illinois; 7. Fred Smalls, LB, West Virginia; 8. Mike Perrino, T, Notre Dame; 9. Mike Zordich, DB, Penn State; 11. Chuck Sanders, RB, Slippery Rock, Pa.; 11a. Drew Smetana, T, Oregon; 12. Jeff Sprowls, DB, Brigham Young; 12a. Mike Travis, DB, Georgia Tech.

San Francisco 49ers

2. Larry Roberts, DE, Alabama; 3. Tom Rathman, RB, Nebraska; 3. Tim McKyer, DB, Texas-Arlington; 3b. John Taylor, WR, Delaware State; 4. Charles Haley, LB, James Madison; 4a. Steve Wallace, T, Auburn; 4b. Kevin Fagan, DT, Miami; 5. Patrick Miller, LB, Florida; 6. Don Griffin, DB, Middle Tennessee; 8. Jim Popp, TE, Vanderbilt; 9. Tony Cherry, RB, Oregon; 10. Ellis-

ton Stinson, WR, Rice; 10a. Harold Hallman, LB, Auburn.

Seattle Seahawks

1. John L. Williams, RB, Florida; 3. Patrick Hunter, DB, Nevada-Reno; 5. Bobby Joe Edmonds, WR, Arkansas; 6. Eddie Anderson, DB, Fort Valley State; 7. Paul Miles, RB, Nebraska; 8. Alonzo Mitz, DE, Florida; 9. Mike Black, T, Cal State-Sacramento; 10. Don Fairbanks, DE, Colorado; 11. David Norrie, QB, UCLA; 12. John McVeigh, LB, Miami.

Tampa Bay Buccaneers

1. Bo Jackson, RB, Auburn; 1a. Roderick Jones, DB, Southern Methodist; 2. Jackie Walker, LB, Jackson State; 2a. Kevin Murphy, LB, Oklahoma; 4. Craig Swoope, DB, Illinois; 5. J.D. Maarleveld, T, Maryland; 6. Kevin Walker, DB, East Carolina; 9. Tommy Barnhardt, P, North Carolina; 10. Benton Reed, DE, Mississippi; 11. Mark Drenth, T, Purdue; 12. Clay Miller, G, Michigan; 12. Mike Crawford, RB, Arizona State.

Washington Redskins

2. Markus Koch, DE, Boise State; 2a. Walter Murray, WR, Hawaii; 3. Alvin Walton, DB, Kansas; 5. Ravin Caldwell, LB, Arkansas; 6. Mark Rypien, QB, Washington State; 6. Jim Huddleston, G, Virginia; 7. Rick Badanjek, RB, Maryland; 8. Kurt Gouveia, LB, Brigham Young; 9. Wayne Asberry, DB, Texas A&M; 11. Kenny Fells, RB, Henderson, Ark.; 12. Eric Yarber, WR, Idaho.

1985 Statistics

Leading Rushers	Att.	Yards	Avg.	Long	TDs
AFC					
Allen, Raiders	380	1759	4.6	161	11
McNeill, Jets	294	1331	4.5	69	3
C. James, N.E.	263	1227	4.7	165	5
Mack, Clev.	222	1104	5.0	61	7
Warner, Sea.	291	1094	3.8	38	8
Byner, Clev.	244	1002	4.1	36	8
Pollard, Pitt.	233	991	4.3	56	3
Brooks, Cin.	192	929	4.8	39	7
Bell, Buff.	223	883	4.0	77	8
McMillan, Ind.	190	858	4.5	38	7
Abercrombie, Pitt.	227	851	3.7	32	7
Wonsley, Ind.	138	716	5.2	36	6
Kinnebrew, Cin.	170	714	4.2	29	9
Winder, Den.	199	714	3.6	42	8
Nathan, Mia.	143	667	4.7	22	5
Collins, N.E.	163	657	4.0	28	3
Heard, K.C.	164	595	3.6	33	4
Hector, Jets	145	572	3.9	22	6
James, S.D.	105	516	4.9	56	2
Spencer, S.D.	124	478	3.9	24	10
NFC					
Riggs, Atl.	397	1719	4.3	50	10
Payton, Chi.	324	1551	4:8	40	9

Leading Rushers	Att.	Yards	Avg.	Long	TDs
Morris, Giants	294	1336	4.5	65	21
Dorsett, Dall.	305	1307	4.3	60	7
Wilder, T.B.	365	1300	3.6	28	10
Dickerson, Rams	292	1234	4.2	43	12
Rogers, Wash.	231	1093	4.7	35	7
Craig, S.F.	214	1050	4.9	62	9
E. Jackson, Phil.	282	1028	3.6	59	5
Mitchell, St. L.	183	1006	5.5	64	7
Nelson, Minn.	200	893	4.5	37	5
J. Jones, Det.	244	886	3.6	29	6
Tyler, S.F.	171	867	5.1	30	6
Riggins, Wash.	176	677	3.8	51	8
W. Wilson, N.O.	168	645	3.8	41	1
Campbell, N.O.	158	643	4.1	45	1
Ivery, G.B.	132	636	4.8	34	2
Clark, G.B.	147	633	4.3	80	5
Ellis, G.B.	104	571	5.5	39	5
Adams, Giants	128	498	3.9	39	2

Leading Passers	Att.	Comp.	Yds. Gnd.	TD Pass	Int.	Rating
AFC						
O'Brien, Jets	488	297	3888	25	8	96.2
Esiason, Cin.	431	251	3443	27	12	93.2
Fouts, S.D.	430	254	3638	27	20	88.1
Marino, Mia.	567	336	4137	30	21	84.1
Kenney, K.C.	338	181	2536	17	9	83.6
Krieg, Sea.	532	285	3602	27	20	76.2
Malone, Pitt.	233	117	1428	13	7	75.5
Elway, Den.	605	327	3891	22	23	70.2
Kosar, Clev.	248	124	1578	8	7	69.3
Moon, Hou.	377	200	2709	15	19	68.5
Eason, N.E.	299	168	2156	11	17	67.5
Pagel, Ind.	393	199	2414	14	15	65.8
Wilson, Raiders	388	193	2608	16	21	62.7
Mathison, Buff.	228	113	1635	4	14	53.5

Leading Passers	Att.	Comp.	Yds. Gnd.	TD Pass	Int.	Rat- ing
NFC						
Montana, S.F	494	303	3653	27	13	91.3
McMahon, Chi.	313	178	2392	15	11	82.6
Brock, Rams	365	218	2658	16	13	82.0
D. White, Dall.	450	267	3157	21	17	80.6
Lomax, St. L.	471	265	3214	18	12	79.5
Simms, Giants	495	275	3829	22	20	78.6
Hipple, Det.	406	223	2952	17	18	73.6
DeBerg, T.B.	370	197	2488	19	18	71.3
Dickey, G.B.	314	172	2206	15	17	70.4
Jaworski, Phil.	484	255	3450	17	20	70.2
Kramer, Minn.	506	277	3522	19	26	67.8
D. Wilson, N.O.	293	145	1843	11	15	60.7
Theismann, Wash.	301	167	1774	8	16	59.6
Archer, Atl.	312	161	1992	7	17	56.5
Ferragamo, Buff.-G.B. ..	287	149	1677	5	17	50.8

Leading Receivers	No.	Yards	Avg.	TDs
AFC				
James, S.D. (RB)	86	1027	11.9	6
Christensen, Raiders	82	987	12.0	6
Woolfolk, Hou. (RB)	80	814	10.2	4
Largent, Sea.	79	1287	16.3	6
Shuler, Jets	76	879	11.6	7
Stallworth, Pitt.	75	937	12.5	5
Nathan, Mia. (RB)	72	651	9.0	1
Clayton, Mia.	70	996	14.2	4
Chandler, S.D.	67	1199	17.9	10
Allen, Raiders (RB)	67	555	8.3	3
Collinsworth, Cin.	65	1125	17.3	5
Hill, Hou.	64	1169	18.3	9
Newsome, Clev.	62	711	11.5	5
Watson, Den.	61	915	15.0	5

Leading Receivers	No.	Yards	Avg.	TDs
NFC				
Craig, S.F. (RB)	92	1016	11.0	6
Monk, Wash.	91	1226	13.5	2
Hill, Dall.	74	1113	15.0	7
Quick, Phil.	73	1247	17.1	11
Clark, Wash.	72	926	12.9	5
Lofton, G.B.	69	1153	16.7	4
Jordan, Minn.	68	795	11.7	0
Cosbie, Dall.	64	793	12.4	6
Spagnola, Phil.	64	772	12.1	5
B. Johnson, Atl.	62	830	13.4	5
Renfro, Dall.	60	955	15.9	8
Ellard, Rams	54	811	15.0	5
Clark, S.F.	54	705	13.1	10
Wilder, T.B. (RB)	53	341	6.4	0

Leading Interceptors	No.	Yards	Long	TDs
AFC				
Lewis, K.C.	8	59	16	0
Daniel, Ind.	8	53	29	0
Marion, N.E.	7	189	83	0
Griffin, Cin.	7	116	33	1
Cherry, K.C.	7	87	47	1
Romes, Buff.	7	56	21	0
Harris, Sea.	7	20	17	0
NFC				
Walls, Dall.	9	31	19	0
Castille, T.B.	7	49	20	0
Frazier, Chi.	6	119	33	1
Patterson, Giants	6	88	29	1
Green, Rams	6	84	41	1
Irvin, Rams	6	83	34	1
Lott, S.F.	6	68	25	0
Waymer, N.O.	6	49	28	0
Hopkins, Phil.	6	36	24	1

Leading Scorers, Kicking	PAT	FG	TP
AFC			
Anderson, Pitt.	40/40	33/42	139
Leahy, Jets	43/45	26/34	121
Breech, Cin.	48/50	24/33	120
Reveiz, Mia.	50/52	22/27	116
Franklin, N.E.	40/41	24/30	112
Karlis, Den.	41/44	23/38	110
Lowery, K.C.	35/35	24/27	107
Thomas, S.D.	51/55	18/28	105
Bahr, Raiders	40/42	20/32	100
Zendejas, Hou.	29/31	21/27	92
NFC			
Butler, Chi.	51/51	31/37	144
Andersen, N.O.	27/29	31/35	120
Murray, Det.	31/33	26/31	109
Lansford, Rams	38/39	22/29	104
McFadden, Phil.	29/29	25/30	104
Luckhurst, Atl.	29/29	24/31	101
Septien, Dall.	42/43	19/28	99
Moseley, Wash.	31/33	22/34	97
Igwebulke, T.B.	30/32	22/32	96
Del Greco, G.B.	38/40	19/26	95

Leading Scorers, Touchdowns	TDs	Rush	Rec.	Ret.	TP
AFC					
Lipps, Pitt.	15	1	12	2	90
Allen, Raiders	14	11	3	0	84
Davenport, Mia.	13	11	2	0	78
Turner, Sea.	13	0	13	0	78
Brooks, Cin.	12	7	5	0	72
Bryner, Clev.	10	8	2	0	60
Chandler, S.D.	10	0	10	0	60
Fryar, N.E.	10	1	7	2	60
Kinnebrew, Cin.	10	9	1	0	60
Mack, Clev.	10	7	3	0	60

Leading Scorers, Touchdowns	TDs	Rush	Rec.	Ret.	TP
Paige, Jets	10	8	2	0	60
Paige, K.C.	10	0	10	0	60
Spencer, S.D.	10	10	0	0	60
NFC					
Morris, Giants	21	21	0	0	126
Craig, S.F.	15	9	6	0	90
Dickerson, Rams	12	12	0	0	72
Payton, Chi.	11	9	2	0	66
Quick, Phil.	11	0	11	0	66
Brown, Minn.	10	7	3	0	60
Clark, S.F.	10	0	10	0	60
Dorsett, Dall.	10	7	3	0	60
Mitchell, St. L.	10	7	3	0	60
Riggs, Atl.	10	10	0	0	60
Wilder, T.B.	10	10	0	0	60

Leading Punters	No.	Yards	Long	Avg.
AFC				
Stark, Ind.	78	3584	68	45.9
Roby, Mia.	59	2576	63	43.7
Camarillo, N.E.	92	3953	75	43.0
Mojsiejenko, S.D.	68	2881	67	42.4
McInally, Cin.	57	2410	64	42.3
L. Johnson, Hou.	83	3464	65	41.7
Kidd, Buff.	92	3818	67	41.5
J. Arnold, K.C.	93	3827	62	41.2
Norman, Den.	92	3764	61	40.9
Guy, Raiders	89	3627	68	40.8
Finzer, Sea.	68	2766	61	40.7
Gossett, Clev.	81	3261	64	40.3
Jennings, Jets	74	2978	66	40.2
Newsome, Pitt.	78	3088	59	39.6
NFC				
Donnelly, Atl.	59	2574	68	43.6
Hatcher, Rams	87	3761	67	43.2

Leading Punters	No.	Yards	Long	Avg.
Landeta, Giants	81	3472	68	42.9
Coleman, Minn.	67	2867	62	42.8
Hansen, N.O.	89	3763	58	42.3
Buford, Chi.	68	2870	69	42.2
Garcia, T.B.	77	3233	61	42.0
Saxon, Dall.	81	3396	57	41.9
Black, Det.	73	3054	60	41.8
Cox, Wash.	52	2175	57	41.8
Birdsong, St. L.	85	3545	67	41.7
Horan, Phil.	91	3777	75	41.5
Runager, S.F.	86	3422	57	39.8
Prokop, G.B.	56	2210	66	39.5

Leading Punt Returners	No.	Yards	Avg.	TDs
AFC				
Fryar, N.E.	37	520	14.1	2
Lipps, Pitt.	36	437	12.1	2
Walker, Raiders	62	692	11.2	0
Martin, Ind.	40	443	11.1	1
Skansi, Sea.	31	312	10.1	0
Drewrey, Hou.	24	215	9.0	0
Vigorito, Mia.	22	197	9.0	0
Lane, K.C.	43	381	8.9	0
V. Johnson, Den.	30	260	8.7	0
James, S.D.	25	213	8.5	0
NFC				
Ellard, Rams	37	501	13.5	1
J. Smith, St. L.	26	283	10.9	0
Mandley, Det.	38	403	10.6	1
Jenkins, Wash.	26	272	10.5	0
Cooper, Phil.	43	364	8.5	0
McConkey, Giants	53	442	8.3	0
Taylor, Chi.	25	198	7.9	0
Bates, Dall.	22	152	6.9	0
McLemore, S.F.	38	258	6.8	0
Allen, Atl.	21	141	6.7	0

Leading Kickoff Returners	No.	Yards	Avg.	TDs
AFC				
Young, Clev.	35	898	25.7	0
Bentley, Ind.	27	674	25.0	0
Drewrey, Hou.	26	642	24.7	0
V. Johnson, Den.	30	740	24.7	0
Martin, Cin.	48	1104	23.0	0
Spencer, Pitt.	27	617	22.9	0
Hampton, Mia.	45	1020	22.7	0
Walker, Raiders	21	467	22.2	0
James, S.D.	36	779	21.6	0
D. Wilson, Buff.	22	465	21.1	0
NFC				
Brown, Rams	28	918	32.8	3
Gault, Chi.	22	577	26.2	1
Monroe, S.F.	28	717	25.6	1
Rhymes, Minn.	53	1345	25.4	0
Jenkins, Wash.	41	1018	24.8	0
Hall, Det.	39	886	22.7	0
Freeman, T.B.	48	1085	22.6	0
Hunter, Phil.	48	1047	21.8	0
Austin, Atl.	39	838	21.5	1
Tullis, N.O.	23	480	20.9	0

1986
NFL Schedule

Sunday, September 7
Atlanta at New Orleans
Cincinnati at Kan. City
Cleveland at Chicago
Detroit at Minnesota
Houston at Green Bay
Indianapolis at New Eng.
L.A. Raiders at Denver
L.A. Rams at St. Louis
Miami at San Diego
N.Y. Jets at Buffalo
Philadelphia at Wash.
Pittsburgh at Seattle
San Fran. at Tampa Bay

Monday, September 8
N.Y. Giants at Dallas

Thursday, September 11
New England at N.Y. Jets

Sunday, September 14
Buffalo at Cincinnati
Cleveland at Houston
Dallas at Detroit
Green Bay at New Orleans
Indianapolis at Miami
Kansas City at Seattle
L.A. Raiders at Wash.
Minnesota at Tampa Bay
Philadelphia at Chicago
St. Louis at Atlanta
San Diego at N.Y. Giants
San Fran. at L.A. Rams

Monday, September 15
Denver at Pittsburgh

Thursday, September 18
Cincinnati at Cleveland

Sunday, September 21
Atlanta at Dallas
Denver at Philadelphia
Houston at Kansas City
L.A. Rams at Indianap.
Miami at N.Y. Jets
New Orleans at San Fran.
N.Y. Giants at L.A. Raiders
Pittsburgh at Minnesota
St. Louis at Buffalo
Seattle at New England
Tampa Bay at Detroit
Washington at San Diego

Monday, September 22
Chicago at Green Bay

Sunday, September 28
Atlanta at Tampa Bay
Chicago at Cincinnati
Detroit at Cleveland
Green Bay at Minnesota
Kansas City at Buffalo
L.A. Rams at Phil.
New England at Denver
New Orl. at N.Y. Giants
N.Y. Jets at Indianap.
Pittsburgh at Houston

San Diego at L.A. Raiders
San Francisco at Miami
Seattle at Washington

Monday, September 29
Dallas at St. Louis

Sunday, October 5
Buffalo at N.Y. Jets
Cincinnati vs. Green Bay
   at Milwaukee
Cleveland at Pittsburgh
Dallas at Denver
Houston at Detroit
Indianapolis at San Fran.
L.A. Raiders at Kan. City
Miami at New England
Minnesota at Chicago
N.Y. Giants at St. Louis
Philadelphia at Atlanta
Tampa Bay at L.A. Rams
Washington at New Orl.

Monday, October 6
San Diego at Seattle

Sunday, October 12
Buffalo at Miami
Chicago at Houston
Denver at San Diego
Detroit at Green Bay
Kansas City at Cleveland
L.A. Rams at Atlanta
Minnesota at San Fran.
New Orleans at Indianap.
N.Y. Jets at New England
Philadelphia at N.Y. Giants
St. Louis at Tampa Bay
Seattle at L.A. Raiders
Washington at Dallas

Monday, October 13
Pittsburgh at Cincinnati

Sunday, October 19
Chicago at Minnesota
Dallas at Philadelphia
Detroit at L.A. Rams
Green Bay at Cleveland
Houston at Cincinnati
Indianapolis at Buffalo
L.A. Raiders at Miami
New England at Pittsburgh
N.Y. Giants at Seattle
St. Louis at Washington
San Diego at Kansas City
San Francisco at Atlanta
Tampa Bay at New Orleans

Monday, October 20
Denver at N.Y. Jets

Sunday, October 26
Atlanta at L.A. Rams
Cincinnati at Pittsburgh
Cleveland at Minnesota
Detroit at Chicago
L.A. Raiders at Houston
Miami at Indianapolis
New England at Buffalo
New Orleans at N.Y. Jets
St. Louis at Dallas
San Diego at Phil.
San Fran. vs. Green Bay
   at Milwaukee
Seattle at Denver
Tampa Bay at Kansas City

Monday, October 27
Washington at N.Y. Giants

Sunday, November 2
Atlanta at New England

Buffalo at Tampa Bay
Cincinnati at Detroit
Cleveland at Indianap.
Dallas at N.Y. Giants
Denver at L.A. Raiders
Green Bay at Pittsburgh
Houston at Miami
Kansas City at San Diego
Minnesota at Washington
N.Y. Jets at Seattle
Philadelphia at St. Louis
San Fran. at New Orleans

Monday, November 3
L.A. Rams at Chicago

Sunday, November 9
Chicago at Tampa Bay
Cincinnati at Houston
L.A. Raiders at Dallas
L.A. Rams at New Orleans
Minnesota at Detroit
New England at Indianap.
N.Y. Giants at Philadelphia
N.Y. Jets at Atlanta
Pittsburgh at Buffalo
St. Louis at San Fran.
San Diego at Denver
Seattle at Kansas City
Washington at Green Bay

Monday, November 10
Miami at Cleveland

Sunday, November 16
Chicago at Atlanta
Cleveland at L.A. Raiders
Dallas at San Diego
Detroit at Philadelphia
Houston at Pittsburgh
Indianapolis at N.Y. Jets
Kansas City at Denver

New England at L.A. Rams
Miami at Buffalo
N.Y. Giants at Minnesota
New Orleans at St. Louis
Seattle at Cincinnati
Tampa Bay vs. Green Bay
   at Milwaukee

Monday, November 17
San Francisco at Wash.

Thursday, November 20
L.A. Raiders at San Diego

Sunday, November 23
Atlanta at San Francisco
Buffalo at New England
Dallas at Washington
Denver at N.Y. Giants
Detroit at Tampa Bay
Green Bay at Chicago
Indianapolis at Houston
Kansas City at St. Louis
Minnesota at Cincinnati
New Orleans at L.A. Rams
Philadelphia at Seattle
Pittsburgh at Cleveland

Monday, November 24
N.Y. Jets at Miami

Thursday, November 27
Green Bay at Detroit
Seattle at Dallas

Sunday, November 30
Atlanta at Miami
Buffalo at Kansas City
Cincinnati at Denver
Houston at Cleveland
L.A. Rams at N.Y. Jets
New England at New Orl.

Phil. at L.A. Raiders
Pittsburgh at Chicago
San Diego at Indianap.
Tampa Bay at Minnesota
Washington at St. Louis

Monday, December 1
N.Y. Giants at San Fran.

Sunday, December 7
Cincinnati at New Eng.
Cleveland at Buffalo
Dallas at L.A. Rams
Denver at Kansas City
Detroit at Pittsburgh
Houston at San Diego
Indianapolis at Atlanta
Miami at New Orleans
Minnesota at Green Bay
N.Y. Giants at Washington
N.Y. Jets at San Francisco
St. Louis at Philadelphia
Tampa Bay at Chicago

Monday, December 8
L.A. Raiders at Seattle

Saturday, December 13
Pittsburgh at N.Y. Jets
Washington at Denver

Sunday, December 14
Buffalo at Indianapolis
Cleveland at Cincinnati

Green Bay at Tampa Bay
Kan. City at L.A. Raiders
Miami at L.A. Rams
Minnesota at Houston
New Orleans at Atlanta
Philadelphia at Dallas
St. Louis at N.Y. Giants
San Fran. at New England
Seattle at San Diego

Monday, December 15
Chicago at Detroit

Friday, December 19
L.A. Rams at San Fran.

Saturday, December 20
Denver at Seattle
Green Bay at N.Y. Giants

Sunday, December 21
Atlanta at Detroit
Buffalo at Houston
Chicago at Dallas
Indianap. at L.A. Raiders
Kan. City at Pittsburgh
New Orleans at Minnesota
N.Y. Jets at Cincinnati
San Diego at Cleveland
Tampa Bay at St. Louis
Washington at Phil.

Monday, December 22
New England at Miami

BRUCE WEBER PICKS
HOW THEY'LL FINISH IN 1986

AFC East

1. Miami
2. New York
3. New England
4. Indianapolis
5. Buffalo

AFC Central

1. Cincinnati
2. Cleveland
3. Pittsburgh
4. Houston

AFC West

1. Los Angeles
2. Denver
3. San Diego
4. Seattle
5. Kansas City

NFC East

1. New York
2. Washington
3. Dallas
4. Philadelphia
5. St. Louis

NFC Central

1. Chicago
2. Detroit
3. Green Bay
4. Minnesota
5. Tampa Bay

NFC West

1. San Francisco
2. Los Angeles
3. New Orleans
4. Atlanta

AFC Champions: Los Angeles Raiders

NFC Champions: New York Giants

Super Bowl Champions: Los Angeles Raiders

YOU PICK
HOW THEY'LL FINISH IN 1986

AFC East

1. New England
2. Miami
3. New York
4. Buffalo
5. Indianapolis

AFC Central

1. Cleveland
2. Cincinati
3. Pittsburgh
4. Houston

AFC West

1. Denver
2. San Diego
3. Seattle
4. Los Angles
5. Kansas City

NFC East

1. Washington
2. New York
3. Philadelphia
4. Dallas
5. St. Louis

NFC Central

1. Chicago
2. Detroit
3. Minnesota
4. Green Bay
5. Tampa Bay

NFC West

1. Los Angles
2. San Francisco
3. Atlanta
4. New Orleans

AFC Champions: Denver
NFC Champions: Chicago
Super Bowl Champions: Denver